PENGUIN BOOKS
THE INDIANS

Sudhir Kakar is an internationally renowned psychoanalyst and writer. He has been a visiting professor at the universities of Chicago, Harvard, McGill, Melbourne, Hawaii and Vienna and a Fellow at the Institutes of Advanced Study, Princeton and Berlin. Currently, he is Adjunct Professor of Leadership at INSEAD in Fontainbleau, France. His many honours include the Bhabha, Nehru and National Fellowships in India, the Kardiner Award of Columbia University, the Boyer Prize of the American Anthropological Association, and Germany's Goethe Medal. The leading French magazine *Le Nouvel Observateur* listed him as one of twenty-five major thinkers of the world.

Sudhir Kakar's books have been translated into twenty languages around the world. His non-fiction books include *The Inner World: A Psychoanalytical Study of Childhood and Society in India; Intimate Relations: Exploring Indian Sexuality; The Analyst and the Mystic: Psychoanalytic Reflections on Religion and Mysticism* and *The Colours of Violence.* His three published novels are *The Ascetic of Desire, Ecstasy* and *Mira and the Mahatma.* He has also translated (with Wendy Doniger) Vatsyayana's *Kamasutra.* He lives in Goa.

*

Katharina Kakar studied Comparative Religions, Indian Art and Anthropology at the Free University of Berlin. She has taught at the Free University and the College of Protestant Theology, Berlin and was a Fellow at the Centre of the Study of World Religions at Harvard University. She is the author of the books *Hindu-Frauen zwischen Tradition und Moderne (Hindu Women between Tradition and Modernity)* and *Der Gottmensch aus Puttaparthi: Eine Analyse der Sathya-Sai-Baba-Bewegung und ihrer Westlichen Anhänger (The Godman of Puttaparthi: An Analysis of the Sathya-Sai-Baba-Movement and its Western Devotees).*

PRAISE FOR *THE INDIANS*

'This is a book which should be read by all Indian executives'—Mark Tully, *Financial Express*

'This stimulating book is a magnificent attempt to understand Indian life in all its fullness . . . deepens our understanding of not just our lives but our minds as well'—*The Statesman*

'Mr and Mrs Kakar display an encyclopedic and deep understanding of the Indian social reality, their "way of looking at things" is surpassed by none'—*Far Eastern Economic Review*

'This incisive book . . . succeeds in great measure in understanding and explaining the Indian character'—*Deccan Herald*

'Both intellectually rigorous and sensitive, Sudhir Kakar is a reliable guide to how Indians today experience their identity, their sexuality, their conflict between tradition and modernity'—*Le Monde*, France

'A very readable and richly nuanced book which seeks to uncover the common identity of 'The Indians' in their historical continuity, homogeneity and civilizational uniqueness'—*Neue Zuricher Zeitung*, Switzerland

'The fascinating portrait of the society and culture of a country that will play an ever more important role in world politics in the future'—*Die Zeit*, Germany

# THE INDIANS

*Portrait of a People*

SUDHIR KAKAR
KATHARINA KAKAR

PENGUIN BOOKS

PENGUIN BOOKS
Published by the Penguin Group
Penguin Books India Pvt. Ltd, 11 Community Centre, Panchsheel Park,
New Delhi 110 017, India
Penguin Group (USA) Inc., 375 Hudson Street, New York, New York 10014,
USA
Penguin Group (Canada), 90 Eglinton Avenue East, Suite 700, Toronto, Ontario,
M4P 2Y3, Canada (a division of Pearson Penguin Canada Inc.)
Penguin Books Ltd, 80 Strand, London WC2R 0RL, England
Penguin Ireland, 25 St Stephen's Green, Dublin 2, Ireland (a division of Penguin
Books Ltd)
Penguin Group (Australia), 707 Collins Street, Melbourne, Victoria 3008, Australia
(a division of Pearson Australia Group Pty Ltd)
Penguin Group (NZ), 67 Apollo Drive, Rosedale, Auckland 0632, New Zealand
(a division of Pearson New Zealand Ltd)
Penguin Group (South Africa) (Pty) Ltd, 24 Sturdee Avenue, Rosebank, Johannesburg
2196, South Africa

Penguin Books Ltd, Registered Offices: 80 Strand, London WC2R 0RL, England

First published in Viking by Penguin Books India 2007
Published by Penguin Book 2009

Copyright © Sudhir Kakar and Katharina Kakar 2007

10 9 8 7 6 5 4 3

ISBN 9780143066637

This edition is for sale in the Indian Subcontinent only

Typeset in Sabon Roman by SŪRYA, New Delhi
Printed at Repro India Ltd., Navi Mumbai

ALWAYS LEARNING          **PEARSON**

# CONTENTS

**Introduction** 1

**The Hierarchical Man** 7
The Web of Family Life 8
Indian Culture and Authority 13

**The Inner Experience of Caste** 25
Dirt and Discrimination 29

**Indian Women: Traditional and Modern** 41
A Daughter Is Born 42
Discrimination and the Maiden 46
Entering Puberty 52
Marriage: Is Love Necessary? 56
The Home and the World 66

**Sexuality** 71
Sex in Ancient India 71
    Women in the *Kamasutra* 76
    Love in the Age of the *Kamasutra* 78
    Sexuality in the Temples and Literature of Medieval India 81
Contemporary Sexuality 84
    Sexuality and Health 86
    Virgins and Others 89

Sexuality in Marriage  93
A Shadow on Male Sexuality  96
Alternate Sexualities  100

**Health and Healing: Dying and Death  107**
The Body in Health and Illness in Ayurveda  111
A Visit to the Ayurvedic Doctor  115
Food and the Indian Mind  121
Health and Modern Medicine  125
View of Death  128

**Religious and Spiritual Life  134**
The Hindu Nationalist  135
The Flexible Hindu  144

**Conflict: Hindus and Muslims  152**
Hindu Image of the Muslim  156
Muslim Image of the Hindu  159
From Conflict to Violence  162
    The Build-up to Violence  162
    The Role of Religious-Political Demagogues  164
    Rumours and Riots  168
    Moralities of Violence  175
    The Future of Hindu–Muslim Conflict  177

**The Indian Mind  180**
The Hindu World View  180
    Moksha, the Goal of Life  182
    Right and Wrong  185
    Karma, Rebirth and the Indian Mind  193
I and the Other: Separation and Connection  196
Male and Female  201

**Notes and References  204**

**Index  218**

# INTRODUCTION

$O$ur book is about Indian identity. It is about 'Indian-ness', the cultural part of the mind that informs the activities and concerns of the daily life of a vast number of Indians as it guides them through the journey of life. The attitude towards superiors and subordinates, the choice of food conducive to health and vitality, the web of duties and obligations in family life are all as much influenced by the cultural part of the mind as are ideas on the proper relationship between the sexes, or on the ideal relationship with god. Of course, in an individual Indian the civilizational heritage may be modified and overlaid by the specific cultures of his family, caste, class or ethnic group. Yet an underlying sense of Indian identity continues to persist, even into the third or fourth generation in the Indian diasporas around the world—and not only when they gather for a Diwali celebration or to watch a Bollywood movie.

Identity is not a role, or a succession of roles, with which it is often confused. It is not a garment that can be put on or taken off according to the weather outside; it is not 'fluid', but marked by a sense of continuity and sameness irrespective of where the person finds himself during the course of his life. A man's identity—of which the culture that he has grown up in is a vital part—is what makes him recognize himself and *be recognized* by the people who constitute his world. It is not something he has chosen, but something that has seized him. It can hurt, be cursed or bemoaned but cannot be discarded, though it can always be concealed from others or, more tragic, from one's own self.

The cultural part of our personal identity, modern neuroscience tell us, is wired into our brains. The culture in which an infant grows up constitutes the software of the brain, much of which is already in place by the end of childhood. Not that the brain, a social and cultural organ as much as a biological one, does not keep changing with interactions with the environment in later life. Like the proverbial river one never steps into twice, one also never uses the same brain twice. Even if our genetic endowment were to determine fifty per cent of our psyche and early childhood experiences another thirty per cent, there is still a remaining twenty per cent that changes through the rest of our lives. Yet, as the neurologist and philosopher Gerhard Roth observes, 'Irrespective of its genetic endowment, a human baby growing up in Africa, Europe or Japan will become an African, a European or a Japanese. And once someone has grown up in a particular culture and, let us say, is twenty years old, he will never acquire a full understanding of other cultures since the brain has passed through the narrow bottleneck of "culturalization".'[1] In other words, the possibilities of 'fluid' and changing identities in adulthood are rather limited and, moreover, rarely touch the deeper layers of the psyche. So, in a sense, we are Spanish or Korean—or Indian—much before we make the choice or identify this as an essential part of our identity.

We are well aware that at first glance the notion of a singular Indian-ness may seem far-fetched. How can anyone generalize about a country of a billion people—Hindus, Muslims, Sikhs, Christians, Jains—speaking fourteen major languages and with pronounced regional differences? How can one postulate anything in common between a people divided not only by social class but also by India's signature system of caste, and with an ethnic diversity characteristic more of past empires than of modern nation states? Yet from ancient times, European, Chinese and Arab travellers have identified common features among India's peoples. They have borne witness to an underlying unity in apparent diversity, a unity often ignored or unseen in recent times because our modern eyes are more attuned to spotting divergence than resemblance. Thus in 300 BC, Megasthenes, the Greek ambassador to Chandragupta Maurya's court, remarked on what one would today call the Indian preoccupation with spirituality:

> Death is with them a frequent subject of discourse. They regard this life as, so to speak, the time when the child within the womb becomes mature, and death as a birth into a real and happy life for the votaries of philosophy. On this account they undergo much discipline as a preparation for death. They consider nothing that befalls men as either good or bad, to suppose otherwise being a dream-like illusion, else how could some be affected with sorrow and others with pleasure by the very same things, and how could the same things affect the same individuals at different times with these opposite emotions?[2]

In more recent times, India's first prime minister, Jawaharlal Nehru, wrote in his *The Discovery of India*:

> The unity of India was no longer merely an intellectual conception for me; it was an emotional experience which overpowered me... It was absurd, of course, to think of India or any country as a kind of anthropomorphic entity. I did not do so... Yet I think with a long cultural background and a common outlook on life develops a spirit that is peculiar to it and that is impressed on all its children, however much they may differ among themselves.[3]

This 'spirit of India' is not something ethereal, inhabiting the rarefied atmosphere of religion, aesthetics and philosophy, but is captured, for instance, in animal fables from the *Panchatantra* or tales from the *Mahabharata* and *Ramayana* that adults tell children all over the country. It shines through Indian musical forms but is also found in mundane matters of personal hygiene such as the cleaning of the rectal orifice with water and the fingers of the left hand, or in such humble objects as the tongue scraper, a curved strip of copper (or silver in the case of the wealthy) used to remove the white film that coats the tongue.

Indian-ness, then, is about similarities produced by an overarching Indic, pre-eminently Hindu civilization that has contributed the lion's share to what we would call the 'cultural gene pool' of India's peoples. In other words, Hindu culture patterns—which are the focus of this book—have played a very major role in the construction of Indian-ness, although we would hesitate to go as far as the acerbic critic of Hindu ethos, the writer Nirad C. Chaudhuri, who maintained that the history of India for the last thousand years has been shaped by the Hindu character and that he felt 'equally certain that it will remain so and shape the form of everything that is being undertaken for and in the country.'[4] Here we can mention only some of the key building blocks of Indian-ness, which we will elaborate upon in this book: an ideology of family and other crucial relationships that derives from the institution of the joint family; a view of social relations profoundly influenced by the institution of caste; an image of the human body and bodily processes that is based on the medical system of Ayurveda; and a cultural imagination teeming with shared myths and legends, especially from the epics *Ramayana* and *Mahabharata*, that underscore a 'romantic' vision of human life and a relativist, context-dependent way of thinking.

We do not mean to imply that Indian identity is a fixed

constant, unchanging through the march of history. Indic
civilization has remained in constant ferment through the
processes of assimilation, transformation, re-assertion and re-
creation that happened in the wake of its encounters with
other civilizations and cultural forces, such as those that came
with the advent of Islam in medieval times and European
colonialism in the more recent past. Virtually no part of Indic
civilization has remained unaffected by these encounters, be it
classical music, architecture, 'traditional' Indian cuisine or
Bollywood musical scores. Indic civilization has not so much
absorbed as translated foreign cultural forces into its own
idiom, unmindful or even oddly proud of all that is lost in
translation. The contemporary buffeting of this civilization by
a West-centric globalization is only the latest in a long line of
invigorating cultural encounters that can be called 'clashes'
only from the shortest of time frames and narrowest of
perspectives. Indic civilization, as separate from though related
to Hinduism as a religion, is thus the common patrimony of all
Indians, irrespective of their professed faith.

Indians, then, share a family resemblance in the sense that
there is a distinctive Indian stamp on certain universal
experiences which we shall discuss in this book: growing up
male or female, sex and marriage, behaviour at work, status
and discrimination, the body in illness and health, religious life
and, finally, ethnic conflict. In a contentious Indian polity,
where various groups clamour for recognition of their
differences, the awareness of a common Indian-ness, the sense
of 'unity within diversity', is often absent. Like the Argentinian
writer Jorge Luis Borges' remark on the absence of camels in
the Quran because they were not exotic enough to the Arabs
to merit attention, the camel of Indian-ness is invisible to or
taken for granted by most Indians. Their 'family' resemblance
begins to stand out in sharp relief only when it is compared to
the profiles of peoples of other major civilizations or cultural

clusters. A man who is an 'Amritsari' in Punjab, for instance, is a Punjabi in the rest of India but an Indian in Europe; in the latter case, the 'outer circle' of his identity—his Indian-ness—becomes central to his self-definition and his recognition by others.[5] This is why in spite of persistent academic disapproval, people (including academics in their unguarded moments) continue to speak of 'the Indians'—as they do of 'the Chinese', 'the Europeans' or 'the Americans'—as a necessary and legitimate short cut to a more complex reality.

Our aim in this book is to present a composite portrait in which Indians will recognize themselves and be recognized by others. This recognition cannot have a uniform quality even while we seek to identify the commonalities that underlie what the anthropologist Robin Fox calls the 'dazzle' of surface differences. We suspect that Hindus belonging to the upper and middle castes will see a picture in which they will find many features that are intimately familiar. Others at the margins of Hindu society (such as the dalits and tribals, or the Christians and Muslims) will spot only fleeting resemblances. Even in the case of Hindus, who constitute over eighty per cent of India's population, the portrait is not a photograph. But neither is it a cubist representation à la Picasso where the subject is barely recognizable. Our effort is more akin to the psychological studies of such expressionist painters as Max Beckman and Oskar Kokoschka or, nearer to our times, the portraits of Lucien Freud that use realism to explore psychological depth.

We are also aware that what we are attempting here is an unfashionable 'big picture', a 'grand narrative' that may be regarded with reflexive hostility by many who profess the postmodernist credo. Yes, there *is* a speculative quality in this exercise of settling on certain patterns of Indian-ness as central. Yet without the big picture—whatever its flaws of inexactness—the smaller, local pictures, however accurate, will be myopic, a mystifying jumble of trees without the pattern of the forest.

# THE HIERARCHICAL MAN

*I*n an article titled 'Where rank alone matters', the well-known Indian journalist Sunanda K. Datta-Ray writes that the gratification of 300 million middle-class consumers, the 'new brahmins', does not lie in their being consumers in a global marketplace but in being 'somebody' in a profoundly hierarchical society.[1] Retired judges, ex-ambassadors and other sundry officials of the Indian state who are no longer in service are never caught without calling cards prominently displaying who they once were. India is not a country for the anonymous, he concludes. You must be *somebody* to survive with dignity, since rank is the only substitute for money. He could have added that India also provides by far the largest number of aspirants for the Guinness Book of Records. The Indian ingenuity in finding ever new fields for setting records (and we are not talking about the well-known ones for the longest fingernails or the largest moustache) is remarkable, amusing, and oddly touching. Commercially astute British and American publishers of biographical dictionaries and compendia of 'Who's Who'—a lucrative branch of vanity publishing—have discovered that India provides the biggest market for people wanting to be included in such publications which are then prominently displayed in the living room of their homes.

The need to be noticed, to stand out from an anonymous mass, is, of course, not uniquely Indian but a part of the narcissistic heritage of all human beings. What makes this phenomenon particularly ubiquitous—and poignant—in India is that a person's self-worth is almost exclusively determined by the rank he (alone or as part of a family) occupies in the profoundly hierarchical nature of Indian society. If the perception of another person has first to do with gender ('Is this individual male or female?'), followed by age ('Is he/she young or old?') and by other such markers of identity, then in India the determination of relative rank ('Is this person superior or inferior to me?') remains very near the top of subconscious questions evoked in an interpersonal encounter. Indians are perhaps the world's most undemocratic people, living in the world's largest and most plural democracy.

The deeply internalized hierarchical principle, the lens through which men and women in India view their social world, has its origins in the earliest years of a child's life in the family. Indeed, a grasp of the psychological dynamics of family life is vital not only for understanding Indian behaviour towards authority but also in a wide variety of other social situations.

### THE WEB OF FAMILY LIFE

The Indian family: large and noisy, with parents and children, uncles, aunts and sometimes cousins, presided over by benevolent grandparents, all of them living together under a single roof. There are intrigues and secret liaisons, fierce loving and jealous rages. Its members often squabble among themselves but remain, in most cases, intensely loyal to each other and always present a united front to the outside world. The Indian family—animated with such a powerful sense of life that a separation from it leaves one with a perpetual sense of exile.

This is the 'joint' family of Bollywood movies which, social scientists tell us, has never been a universal norm. It is also untrue that the large joint family is found more often in villages than in cities; studies tell us that it is more common in urban areas, as also among the upper landholding castes, than in the lower castes of rural India. Economic reasons, especially the high cost of urban living space, are certainly a reason why the joint family survives. Contemporary nostalgia at the supposed withering away of the Indian family with the increasing pace of modernization could well be misplaced; the prevalence of joint families may be increasing rather than declining.[2] It is important to note that irrespective of demographic changes and the desire of many modern middle-class couples to escape the tensions of a large family and live on their own, the joint family remains the most desirable form of family organization and has a *psychic reality* independent of its actual occurrence.[3]

What is this 'joint' family that is so much a feature of an Indian's inner landscape, even in places and social strata where it is not the dominant form of family organization any more?[4] As an ideal type, a joint family is one in which brothers remain together after marriage and bring their wives into the parental household. It is governed by the ideals of fraternal loyalty and filial obedience which stipulate common residence and common economic, social and ritual activities. In addition to this core group, there may be others who are either permanent or temporary residents in the household: widowed or abandoned sisters and aunts, or distant male relatives, euphemistically called 'uncles', who have no other family to turn to. In practice, of course, brothers and their families may not share a common kitchen or may live in adjacent houses rather than in a single residence, or a brother may have migrated to the city in search of economic opportunity. Yet even in cases of many families that appear 'nuclear' in the sense that they are composed of parents and their unmarried children, a social and psychological 'jointness' continues to operate. When a brother moves to the city, for instance, his wife and children frequently continue to live with the village family while he himself remits his share to the family income; or, if he takes his family with him, they return 'home' as often as they can. Even in the upper and upper-middle classes, it is the psychic reality of the joint family which makes them take it for granted that they can visit and live for weeks, if not months, with their adult married children who are working in distant parts of the country or even outside India.

The point we wish to make here is that most Indians spend the formative years of their life in family settings that approximate to the joint rather than the nuclear type. Even grown children who nominally live alone or in a nuclear family make long and frequent visits to members of the joint family. Not only do families get together to celebrate festivals, but people also prefer to go on vacations or on religious pilgrimage in the company of other family members. The ideals of fraternal solidarity and filial devotion are so strong that a constant effort is made to preserve the characteristic 'jointness' at the very least in its social sense. Anyone who has been surprised at the heavy traffic in an Indian city on a late Sunday morning only needs to remember that many of the men, women and children, dressed in their best clothes and precariously perched on scooters, or crammed into buses and small Maruti cars, are on their way to visit family members living in other parts of the city.

In part, the demography of childhood in India reflects Indian marriage patterns. Leaving aside the urban middle and upper classes where the marriageable age has been increasing, most couples marry in adolescence when they have neither the economic nor the psychological resources to set up an independent household. Separation from the joint family, if and when it does take place, comes later, when their own children are well into the middle years of childhood. Thus it is not surprising that uncles, aunts and cousins, not to mention grandparents, figure prominently in the childhood recollections of most Indians. They occupy a much greater space in the inner world of Indians than is the case with Europeans and Americans growing up in nuclear families where it is only the mother and the father (and perhaps also the siblings) who cast such a long shadow on their emotional lives.

More than any other factor, then—the recent high rate of economic growth, the improvement in the status of previously oppressed sections of society and even the strength of religious belief—it is the *family*, and the role family obligations play in the life of an Indian, which is the glue that holds Indian society together. Of course, the flip side of the coin is—and there is always a flip side—that this focus on the family as the exclusive source of satisfaction of *all* one's needs also reflects a continuing lack of faith in almost every other institution of society. The result of this is often extreme divisiveness, a lack of commitment to anyone or anything outside one's immediate family.

In a country without large government programmes of social security, unemployment compensation and old age benefits, the family must give temporary relief when a man loses work, a young mother is ill or monsoon floods destroy the harvest. If we exclude the rising middle class and the very small upper-class elite, it is the family that provides the only life insurance most Indians have. Naturally, then, in the imagination of most Indians a man's worth and, indeed, his identity are inextricable from the reputation of his family. How a man lives and what he does are rarely seen as a product of individual effort or aspiration, but are interpreted in the light of his family's circumstances and standing in the wider society. Individual success or failure makes sense only in a family context. 'How can a son of family X behave like this!' is as much an expression of contempt as 'How could he not turn out well? After all he is the son of family Y!' is a sign of approval.

Psychologically, an individual derives much of his self-esteem from myths that ascribe to his family some kind of distinction or prominence in the past or exaggerate its importance in the present. His closest ties, often including even friendships, will not be outside but within the family. As a Hindu proverb puts it, 'A mustard seed of relationship is worth a cartload of friendship.' These special relationships within the extended family are a major source of support needed to go through life and constant affirmation of a person's identity.

It is not as if family interactions and obligations have been static. Hindu nationalist writings and some women's magazines are full of alarmist stuff about the Indian family being under attack by forces of Western modernization. Many of the changes have to do with the rise of individualism and the role of women in urban areas, to which we will come back later. Family obligations too are changing. Thirty years ago it was taken for granted that a man would look after a cousin or a nephew if he came and stayed with him for many years of schooling which was not available in his home town or village. Most middle-class families will now hesitate to put themselves out to the same extent. Yet, while there has certainly been a contraction of family obligations, they have not disappeared; one may not feel as obliged to look after a distant aunt but there is no question of not looking after the emotional, social and financial needs of an aged parent. All in all, the Indian family remains distinctive (and distinctly conservative) in its views on marriage, parenthood and the web of mutual responsibilities and obligations within wider ties of kinship.[5]

Unshakeable solidarity between brothers as one of the highest ideals of family life can lead to consequences that may appear odd to a 'modern sensibility' which looks upon the husband–wife couple as the fulcrum of family life. For instance, a man will often tolerate the adulterous relations of his wife with his brother—in the upper classes, mostly by feigning ignorance; the poorer sections of society dispense even with this fig leaf. Thus a cook from the hill state of Uttaranchal once came to his employer asking for leave to go to his village since his wife had just given birth to a son.

'But how can your wife bear a son when you have not been to your village in the last one year?' asked the employer.

'How does that matter?' replied the man. 'My brother is there.'

This may seem like an extreme example, but only because it was explicitly stated. The situation itself is not as uncommon as we would suppose. For a time in Indian social history, the erotic importance of the husband's younger brother—in the sense that he would or could have sexual relations with his elder brother's widow—was officially recognized in the custom of *niyoga*. The custom goes back thousands of years to the sacred Rig Veda, where a man, identified by the commentators as the brother-in-law, is described as extending his hand in promised marriage to a widow inclined to share her husband's funeral pyre.

Though the custom gradually fell into disuse, especially with the prohibition of widow remarriage (it still survives in some communities), the psychological core of niyoga, namely the mutual awareness of a married woman and her younger brother-in-law as potential or actual sexual partners, is very much alive. In psychotherapy practice, middle-class women who are on terms of sexual intimacy with a brother-in-law rarely express any feelings of guilt. Their distress is occasioned more by his leaving home or his impending marriage, which the woman perceives as the end of her sensual and emotional life.

### INDIAN CULTURE AND AUTHORITY

An Indian's sense of his relative familial and social position is so internalized that he qualifies, in Louis Dumont's phrase, as the original *homo hierarchicus*.[6] The internalization of hierarchy coincides with the acquisition of language. There are six basic nursery sounds, a universal baby language used by infants all over the world with only slight variation from one society to another.[7] These 'words' are repeated combinations of the vowel sound 'ah' preceded by different consonants—'dada', 'mama', 'baba', 'nana', 'papa' and 'tata'. Infants repeat these or other closely related sounds over and over, in response to their own babbling and to their parents' modified imitations of their baby sounds. In most Western countries, only a few of these repetitive sounds, for example, 'mama', 'dada' or 'papa', are recognized and repeated by the parents and thus reinforced in the infant. In India, on the contrary, just about *all* of these closely related sounds are repeated and reinforced since each one is a name for various elder kin in the family whom a child must learn to identify with the position that he or she occupies in the family hierarchy. Thus, for example, in Punjabi, *ma* is mother, *mama* is mother's brother, *dada* is father's father, *nana* is mother's father, *chacha* is father's younger brother, *taya* is father's elder brother, *masi* is mother's sister, and so on.

This transformation of basic baby language into names for kinship relations within the extended family is characteristic of all Indian languages. It not only symbolizes the child's manifold relationships with a range of potentially nurturing figures in the older generation but also emphasizes the importance of the child's familiarity with the hierarchy of the family organization. Indians must learn to adapt to the personalities and moods of many authority figures besides their parents quite early in life. Whether the highly developed antenna that makes an Indian almost anticipate the wishes of a superior and adjust his behaviour accordingly should be called 'flexibility' or 'a lack of a firm sense of self' is a cultural value judgement we are unwilling to make. The fact remains that such early experiences in an extended family and the child's early knowledge of when to retreat, when to cajole and when to be stubborn in order to get what he wants also make an Indian a formidable negotiator in later business dealings.

Regardless of personal talents or achievements, or of changes in the circumstances of his own or others' lives, an Indian's relative position in the hierarchy of the family, his obligations to those 'above' him and his expectations of those 'below' him, are immutable and lifelong. Already in childhood he begins to learn that he must look after the welfare of those subordinate to him in the family hierarchy so that they do not suffer either through their own misjudgement or at the hands of outsiders, and that he is reciprocally entitled to their obedience and respect.

Since young people in Indian families generally receive a good deal of attention and nurturance from the older generation and maintenance of family integrity is valued higher than an unfolding of individual capacities, a young Indian neither seeks a radical demarcation from the generation of his parents nor feels compelled to overthrow their authority in order to 'live life on my own terms'. This is in stark contrast to the West where 'generational conflict' is not only expected but considered necessary for the renewal of a society's institutions and, moreover, is considered (we believe erroneously) to be a universally valid psychological truth. In India, it is not the rupture but the *stretching* of traditional values that becomes a means for the young person to realize his dreams for life. It is telling that in spite of their fascination with sport and cinema stars, and the omnipresence of these celebrities in advertising, the primary role models for a large majority of Indian youth are from the family, most often a parent.

In spite of rapid social changes in the last decades, an Indian continues to be part of a hierarchically ordered and, above all, stable network of relationships throughout the course of his life. This complex, relationship-based pattern of behaviour also manifests itself in work situations. Although intellectually the Indian professional or bureaucrat may agree with his Western counterpart that, for instance, the criterion for appointment or promotion to a particular job must be objective, a decision based solely on the demands of the task and 'merits of the case', emotionally he must still struggle against the cultural conviction that his relationship to the individual under consideration (if there is one) is the singlemost important factor in his decision. And among the vast majority of traditional-minded countrymen—whether it be a trader bending the law to facilitate the business transaction of a fellow caste member, or an industrialist employing an insufficiently qualified but distantly related job applicant as a manager, or the clerk in the municipal office accepting bribes in order to put an orphaned niece through school—dishonesty, nepotism and corruption are merely abstract concepts. These negative constructions are irrelevant to the Indian experience, which, from childhood on, nurtures one, and only one, standard of responsible adult conduct—namely, an individual's lifelong obligation to his kith and kin. Guilt and its attendant anxiety are aroused only when individual actions go against the principle of primacy of relationships, not when 'foreign', different ethical standards of honesty, equity and justice are breached.

Although family relationships are hierarchical in structure, the mode of relationship is characterized by an almost maternal behaviour on the part of the superior, by filial respect and compliance on the part of the subordinate and by a mutual sense of highly personal attachment. We meet this kind of a superior—king, father, guru—in school textbooks where, in stories depicting authority situations, the ideal leader is a kind of benevolent patriarch who acts in a nurturing way so that his followers either anticipate his wishes or accept them without questioning.[8] He receives compliance by taking care of his people's needs, by providing the emotional rewards of approval, praise and affection, or by arousing guilt. High-handed attempts to regulate behaviour through threat or punishment, rejection or humiliation, lead less to open defiance than to devious evasion on the part of the subordinate.

Another legacy of Indian childhood in superior-subordinate or leader-follower relations is the idealization of the former. The need to bestow *maana* on our superiors and leaders in order to partake of this magical power ourselves is an unconscious attempt to restore the narcissistic perfection of infancy: 'You are perfect and I am a part of you.' This is of course a universal tendency, but in India, the automatic reverence for superiors is a widespread psychological fact. Leaders at every level of society, but particularly the patriarchal elders of the extended family and caste groups, as also religious and spiritual leaders, take on an emotional importance independent of any realistic evaluation of their performance, let alone an acknowledgement of their all too human weaknesses. Charisma, then, plays an unusually significant role among Indians and is a vital constituent of effective leadership in institutions.[9] In contrast to most people in the West, Indians are generally more prone to revere than admire.

It is not as if Indians are not sceptical of authority figures. Indeed, their cynicism towards leaders, especially political leaders, is often extreme. It is only that when an Indian *grants* authority to a leader, his critical faculties disappear in the waves of credulity that wash over him. The granting of authority is involuntary in the case of family and caste leadership during childhood. It may be voluntary—to gurus of various hues, for instance—in situations of acute personal crisis or distress, the reason why, for example, healers of the most varied kind flourish in the country. The effectiveness of these healers may be less because of their particular healing regimens and more due to the unconscious vital forces that the healer's charisma mobilizes in the patient in service of a cure.

Do these patterns of family life, especially those connected with the hierarchical ordering of relationships, extend beyond the home into other institutions like university departments, offices, political parties and the bureaucracy? The evidence suggests that they do. Authority relations in the Indian family provide a template for the functioning of most modern business, educational, political and scientific organizations.

First, there is a strong preference for an authoritative, even autocratic (but not authoritarian) leader who is strict, demanding but also caring and nurturing—very much like the *karta*, the paternalistic head of the extended family. The organizational psychologist Jai Sinha has called this type of leader the 'nurturant-task' leader who is strict in getting the task accomplished and tries to dominate the activities of his subordinates.[10] He is, however, not authoritarian but nurturing in the sense of being a benevolent guide to his subordinates and someone who takes a personal interest in their well-being and growth.

Among the subordinates, on the other hand, there is a complementary tendency to idealize the leader and look upon him as a repository of all virtues, an almost superhuman figure deserving of their faith and respect. Even in the upper echelons of modern business organizations, among senior managers with exposure to Western business education and practices, the influence of Indian culture on their perception of top leadership has not disappeared. The CEO of a modern company here is the recipient of far greater idealization than is usually the case in the West.[11] This is a potential strength of Indian organizations and has many advantages, such as a greater *esprit de corps* in senior management and a higher degree of loyalty and commitment to the organization. It can also lead to a work ethic and performance that is much more than what a leader might reasonably expect in most European and North American organizations. Yet idealization, that great construct of human imagination which allows one to conceive with the conviction of a known fact a more perfect and valuable reality than what exists, can also distort the perception of leadership. The Indian leader is thus often deprived of critical feedback from the senior people of his organization that could help him develop more effective leadership practices.

Since Indian institutions are markedly hierarchical, collaborative teamwork across levels of status and power proves to be difficult. Decisions tend to be pushed upwards and the top leadership must often intervene in organizational processes. More than in most Western cultures, the legacy of Indian family and childhood ensures that the quality of leadership becomes pivotal for the success or failure of an institution.

The difficulty in working in teams is compounded by the cultural obstacles to giving or receiving negative feedback. With the preservation of relationships as the primary principle governing their actions in interpersonal situations, Indians find it difficult to say a frank 'No' to requests they are unable or unwilling to grant. The refusal has then to be interpreted from the words in which the rejection is couched ('Let's see' or 'It's difficult but I will try', and so on), and from the tentative tone of voice and cautious body language. One has to exercise the same kind of judgement when asking for directions on an Indian street. The man who might not have an idea of the right directions but nonetheless proceeds to guide you to your destination is not only saving face by not admitting to his ignorance but also hesitates to introduce any negative vibes in the fleeting relationship that has just come into being.

The absence of a democratic mode of functioning in Indian institutions is not resented as long as those in leadership positions develop a close personal relationship with the led. In fact, effective leaders in India, both in the workplace and in the political arena, place great emphasis on the building and cultivating of relationships. This, as we have seen above, is consistent with an Indian's experience from his earliest years where he has learnt that the core of any social relationship—in family, caste, school or at work—is caring and mutual involvement. What he should be sensitive to (and concerned with) are not only the goals of work that are external to the relationship but the relationship itself, the unfolding of emotional affinity.

As in the extended family, where favouritism has to be avoided to maintain harmony (for example, in the ideology of a joint family a father should not be seen as favouring his own son above the sons of his brothers), people in Indian organizations develop almost paranoid abilities in detecting signs of a leader's favouritism toward selected subordinates. Not that they are particularly troubled by nepotism—as long as *they* are the intended beneficiaries. Most accept that people in authority will make a distinction between their 'own people' and those who are not in the same privileged position. They have a sneaking sympathy for a senior politician's incredulous reaction to a journalist who questioned the appointment of the politician's son to a high post within his party: 'Who else will I appoint? *Your* son?' If there is one 'ism' that governs Indian society and its institutions, it is familyism.

Given the strong need for nearness to the superior, to be considered 'his man', what is galling for an Indian is being excluded—or the feeling of being excluded—from a charmed circle that enjoys the superior's favour. The result of this, almost always, is a good deal of hidden anger and passive aggressive behaviour. Effective leaders in Indian institutions are thus constantly on their guard against any impression of favouritism, because it can cause serious damage to the morale of the institution.

Some of the values that govern Indian institutional and work life have been empirically demonstrated by the GLOBE (Global

Leadership and Organizational Behavior Effectiveness) research project, which surveyed over 17,000 middle managers in various industries in sixty-two societies.[12] In this project, the sixty-two countries were grouped into ten cultural clusters: Latin Europe, Germanic Europe, Anglo Europe, Nordic Europe, Eastern Europe, Latin America, Confucian Asia, Anglo (outside Europe), Sub-Saharan Africa, Southern Asia and Middle East.

If one looks at South Asia, where India is by far the largest country, this cultural cluster stands out prominently in three of the nine dimensions of the study. South Asia has the greatest *power distance*, that is, the degree to which the culture's people are separated by power, authority and prestige.[13] In other words, the difference in status between the chief executive and the office peon, the *raja* and the *runk*, is at its maximum in this region (the least is in Nordic Europe, that is, Scandinavia). Irrespective of his educational status and more than in any other culture in the world, an Indian is a *homo hierarchicus*. This is the case even when the modern Indian manager— usually middle-class, college-educated—wishes that it was not so and, as we shall see below, consciously aspires to a reduction in the power distance.

The second dimension on which South Asia stands out in the international comparison is *humane orientation*, that is, the degree to which people are caring, altruistic, generous and kind. (The lowest here is Germanic Europe. Closely related to humane orientation, although as its opposite, is assertiveness, the degree to which the culture's people are assertive, confrontational and aggressive. Here, next only to Scandinavia, South Asia is the least assertive culture; Germanic Europe and Eastern Europe, in that order, are the most aggressive and confrontational.) Combining humane orientation with a high power distance produces the kind of Indian leader we have discussed earlier: authoritative but not autocratic, sometimes despotic perhaps, but generally benevolent.

South Asia also scores the highest on *in-group collectivism*, that is, the degree to which people feel loyalty toward such small groups as their family or circle of friends (Scandinavia, followed by Germanic Europe and North America, scores the least). We have seen that the habit of solidarity with the family group and later with members of one's caste is inculcated in early childhood and is regarded as one of the highest values guiding individual lives. This solidarity has the many economic advantages of informal networks that are based on trust rather than contractual obligations. We have already talked of the high *esprit de corps* when people working in an organization regard themselves as a 'band of brothers' and idealize the leader-father. The danger, of course, is of 'in-groupism', which makes collaboration with other, 'out' groups in large organizations difficult, if not impossible.

This snapshot of Indian leadership practices says little about the changes taking place in modern urban families which will invariably have an impact on Indian institutions. The GLOBE study confirms that what younger managers in India most dearly wish for is a reduction in the power distance between the leader and the led.[14] We believe that leadership on this dimension is indeed in a state of transition. It is not a coincidence that the desired reduction in psychological distance between the leader and the led is congruent with the changes taking place in the father–son relationship in the middle-class family. Let us elaborate.

In traditional India, the father entered his son's life in a big way only in the later years of the boy's childhood. In the early and middle years, the relationship between the two was (and in large parts of the country continues to be) marked by formality and perfunctory daily social contact.[15] In older autobiographical accounts, fathers, whether strict or indulgent, cold or affectionate, are invariably portrayed as distant. The father's guiding voice, a prime element in a man's sense of identity, was diffused among the voices of many older male family members and his individual paternity muffled.

The reasons for a traditional father not taking a demonstratively active role in the upbringing of his son are not difficult to fathom. A traditional father operates under the logic of the joint family. This demands that in order to prevent the building up of nuclear cells within the family that can destroy its cohesion, a father be restrained in the presence of his own child and divide his interest and support equally among his own and his brothers' children. Moreover, as we shall see later in the chapter on sexuality, many a young father was embarrassed to hold his infant child in front of older family members since this fruit of his loins was clear evidence of activity in that particular region.

The second ideology impinging on traditional fathers in India (and in common with other patriarchal societies) is of a gender-based dichotomy in parenting roles and obligations. That is, decided notions of things that men do in the household and others that they don't. Playing with or taking care of their infants is not what fathers do, their major role lies in the disciplining of the child. As a North Indian proverb, addressed to men, pithily puts it: 'Treat a son like a king for the first five years, like a slave for the next ten and like a friend thereafter.'

Of course, behind the requisite façade of aloofness and impartiality, a traditional Indian father may be struggling to express his love for his son. Fatherly love is no less strong in India than in other societies. Even in ancient religious and literary texts, a son is not only instrumental in the fulfilment of a sacred duty but has often been portrayed as a source of intense emotional gratification.[16] Older autobiographical accounts often depict the Indian father as a sensitive man and charged with feelings for his son which he does not openly reveal. Thus in *Autobiography of a Yogi*, Yogananda describes meeting his father after a long separation: 'Father embraced me warmly as I entered our Gurupur home. "You have come," he said tenderly. Two large tears dropped from his eyes. Outwardly undemonstrative, he had never before shown me these external signs of affection. Outwardly the grave father, inwardly he possessed the melting heart of a mother.'[17]

One of the more striking changes associated with modernity and the rise of an urban middle class is the active involvement of fathers in bringing up their infant and little children.[18] Given the intensity and ambivalence of the mother–son connection in the Indian setting, the need for the father's physical touch and guiding voice, his support and often unconscious encouragement for the son's separation from his mother has always been pressing. Modern, generally urban and educated, fathers have begun to provide this early emotional access to the son, not only attenuating the overheated quality of the mother–son bond, but also laying the foundations for a less hierarchical and closer father–son relationship. The early experience of having fathers who are no longer distant and forbidding figures, who are available to both sons and daughters, often as playmates, will, inevitably, change notions of the desirable power distance in institutions and the expectations that young Indians will have of their leaders.

# THE INNER EXPERIENCE OF CASTE

$\mathcal{S}$econd only to the family as a pervasive social dimension of Indian identity is the institution of caste. Although the usage of the term 'caste' is problematic (it derives from the Portuguese *casta*—'race', 'descent'), the term has entered English and other European languages as an expression for the horizontal segmentation of Indian society. Actually, the term 'caste' refers to not one but two institutions: *varna* and *jaati*. Varna (literally, 'colour') is the ancient division of Hindu society into the priest (brahmin), warrior (*kshatriya*), tradesman (*vaishya*) and servant (*shudra*) classes—in that order of ranking—which is encountered in the Vedas and other founding texts of Hinduism. This four-fold classification is still used to locate a person in the wider social space, as when political commentators speak of mobilizing the brahmin, vaishya or the backward castes (as the shudras are now called) to vote in a state election.

However, caste today almost always refers to jaati, which is caste in all the immediacy of daily social relations and occupational specialization. The jaati system is made up of more than three thousand castes. The hierarchical order of these castes is not static but changes from village to village and from one region to another, although one of the brahmin castes will almost always be at the top of the pecking order. Here, we will talk of caste only in the sense of jaati.

Essentially, jaati is a social group to which an individual belongs by birth. And although this is now rapidly changing, a jaati member would usually follow his caste's traditional occupation. His marriage partner even today, in nine cases out of ten, will belong either to his own caste or to the sub-caste group from which he is permitted to choose a spouse. It isn't surprising, then, that besides hierarchy, the restriction of the marriage partner to one's own caste is the second pillar of the caste system. Except in 'modern' Indians, a person's closest friendships too are with members of his own caste. His relations with members of other castes are more formal, governed as they are by unwritten codes prescribing and proscribing relationships between castes.

Although families of a particular caste may live together in the same village, the caste itself extends beyond the confines of any single village. A large, prominent caste may have millions of members and extend over considerable geographical territory, making it a very desirable group for politicians for the purpose of electoral mobilization. In fact, in militantly heightening caste identities Indian democracy may be the third, new pillar, after endogamy and hierarchy, which props up the institution of caste.

Just as the family is the primary foil for a child's budding sense of identity, caste is the next circle in his widening social radius. The caste's values, beliefs, prejudices and injunctions, as well as its distortions of reality, become part of the individual's mind and contents of his conscience. It is his internalized caste norms that define 'right action' or *dharma* for the individual, make him feel good and loved when he lives up to these norms, and anxious and guilty when he transgresses them.

Since an individual's anxiety may also reflect the latent

concerns of his group, knowledge of an Indian's caste, its aspirations and apprehensions, enriches the understanding of his identity formation. For instance, a person's violent outrage provoked by an ostensibly minor slight may not only be the result of an individual problem in 'managing aggression', it may also have its source in a historical resentment shared by his caste as a whole and passed down from generation to generation as part of his caste identity.

If marriage and kinship are its body, then hierarchy is the soul of caste. The ranking of a caste in the social order, and thus the capital of narcissism available to a person for belonging to a particular caste, is generally according to the criteria of purity vs pollution.[1] A caste is ranked high if its way of life is judged to be pure, and low if it is considered to be relatively polluted. A brahmin is the purest (although there will be gradations of purity in the many brahmin castes) and an untouchable, the dalit (literally, 'oppressed'), the most polluted. Although the rankings in between these extremes in a particular village may be bitterly contested, with a caste claiming a purer way of life than what has been ascribed to it, it is generally agreed that purity and pollution are determined by the caste's way of life, in which its diet (for instance, whether vegetarian or meat-eating) and its traditional occupation are the most important elements. Occupations that put the person in touch with death or with bodily substances (the sweeper, the washerman, the barber, the tanner, the cobbler) are considered the most polluted.

The preoccupation of the caste system with high and low has been associated with suffering and humiliation for several millions through the centuries. As the Marathi poet Govindraj puts it, Hindu society is made up of men 'who bow their heads to the kicks from above and who simultaneously give a kick below, never thinking to resist the one or refrain from the other.'[2] The hierarchy is so fine tuned that even a low caste will always find another caste that is inferior to it, thus mitigating some of the narcissistic injury suffered by it at being seen as inferior. Thus, for instance, 'among those lowest scavenging sections which remove night soil there is still a distinction: those who serve in private houses consider themselves higher than those who clean public latrines.'[3]

Caste hierarchy and its associated discrimination are not solely Hindu phenomena. Dumont has noted that no religious movement in India that has opposed caste has ever been successful in the long run.[4] Although not as widespread or harsh as in Hinduism, the hierarchical principle embodied in the caste system has also put its stamp on the social practices of other religions such as Islam, Christianity and Sikhism which have greater claims to egalitarianism. For instance, in the state of Goa, the term 'brahmin Catholic' is commonly used for a person of high status in the Christian community. To give another example, 'noble' (*ashraf*) Muslims, descended from Turks, Arabs and Persians who settled in India during the eight hundred years of Muslim suzerainty, look down upon and discriminate against the vast majority of their 'base' (*ajlaf*) coreligionists whose forefathers were low-caste indigenous converts. Even lower than the ajlaf are the *arzal*, the Muslim counterparts of the untouchables of Hindu society.

One of the major reasons for very few upper-caste Hindus converting to Islam or Christianity over centuries of Muslim and British rule has to do with the strength of their caste identities. In spite of the absence of any prohibition on changing one's religious faith, and the well-known Hindu respect for all manner of theological currents and openness to a wide variety of spiritual beliefs, it was the prospect of being together with untouchable converts in the same congregation that acted as a powerful deterrent to conversion. In contrast, a large number of untouchables converted to Islam, Christianity and, since the 1950s (with the sensational conversion of the dalit leader B.R.

Ambedkar), to Buddhism in order to escape the discriminatory practices of the caste system.

## DIRT AND DISCRIMINATION

A cardinal feature of caste which makes the caste experience different from that of growing up in a clan or a tribe is the phenomenon of untouchability.

The 150 million untouchables, the dalits, of India comprise a number of 'impure' castes which occupy the lowest rungs in the hierarchy of Hindu society. Earlier—and in many parts of rural India even today—the visceral withdrawal bordering on revulsion at a dalit's approach was so strong that the dalits were denied access to temples, thoroughfares and other public spaces. Their housing was segregated, their children not allowed to attend the common village school and their women forbidden to draw water from the public well lest the drinking water become contaminated.

The degradation of a vast number of other human beings to an extent that members of higher castes in parts of rural India recoil not only from their touch but even from their shadow continues to be a matter of great shame for many Indians. Mahatma Gandhi regarded untouchability as the biggest blot on Hindu society and passionately fought for its eradication the whole of his adult life. In a letter to a correspondent who had talked of upper-caste intolerance of the untouchables, he writes: 'I abhor with my whole soul the system which has reduced a large number of Hindus to a level less than that of beasts. The vexed problem would be solved if the poor *panchama* [literally, 'fifth', that is, below the fourth caste of shudra in the varna classification], not to use the word 'untouchable', was allowed to mind his own business. Unfortunately, he has no mind or business he can call his own. Has a beast any mind or business but that of his master? Has a panchama a place he can call his own? He may not walk on the very roads he cleans and pays for by the sweat of his brow. He may not even dress as the others do...It is an abuse of language to say we Hindus extend any toleration towards our panchama brothers. We have degraded them and then have the audacity to use their very degradation against their rise.'⁵

Vigorous social and political movements in the last century, as also the process of urbanization, have considerably mitigated the horrors of untouchability. But they have by no means disappeared. In its issue of 19 September 2005, the news magazine *India Today* carried a report from a village in Orissa where, for the first time, a dalit girl had been admitted to college for higher education. When the eighteen-year-old girl rode a bicycle to college, the upper-caste-dominated village threatened the dalits with social boycott if she did not walk to college instead. According to custom, dalits in this village can only walk barefoot. They are not allowed to take wedding processions through the village or cremate the dead in the common cremation ground. If they are invited to upper-caste weddings, it is only to wash the feet of the wedding guests.

Modern egalitarian ideologies have indeed led to a questioning of the hierarchical principle among sections of society, especially in the lower castes. But these ideologies have not quite succeeded in breaking hierarchy's tenacious hold on the Indian mind. What the egalitarian ideology has undoubtedly accomplished is to increase the hypocrisy, the gulf between private disparagement and a politically correct public stance towards the dalits.

We have already mentioned that most anthropological scholars of Hindu society agree that 'pollution' or 'impurity' is the central organizing principle of the caste system and, hence, also of untouchability. What are the *psychological* roots of a tradition that so demeans and degrades so many Indians? In the only serious psychological study of untouchability, the eminent folklorist Alan Dundes has postulated that in the

Hindu mind, the untouchable is intimately associated with faeces, and the Hindu horror of faeces, instilled by the culture's toilet training, is the 'cause' for the persistence of untouchability.[6] Although we agree with Dundes' exposition on the importance of dirt as the primary psychological moment in the phenomenon of untouchability, we are sceptical about the (Freudian) responsibility of toilet training for this state of affairs. There is no parallel in India, for instance, to the Western scatological fixations in speech. Equivalents of 'Merde!', 'Shit!', 'Scheisse!' are not common expressions of frustration in any Indian language; nor is there any counterpart to 'Asshole!' or 'Arschloch!' as a familiar term of abuse that gives vent to infantile rage—Indians prefer various incestuous possibilities instead. In other words, it is not in India but in European and Anglo-American speech that one hears the long-postponed vengeance of a child forced to control its bowels.

Our own explanation, diverging from Dundes in some respects, would go something like this: translated into the language of psychological experience, to be pure is to be clean while to be polluted is to be dirty. For the upper-caste child, a dalit is a member of a group that is permanently and irrevocably dirty. The child's knowledge is not anthropological or religious-textual but a *knowledge-feeling* that is pre-verbal and has, so to speak, entered the child's very bones. Many a time while growing up, the child has sensed the sudden kinesthetic tension in the body of his mother, father, aunt, uncle, when a dalit has come too near. He has registered their expressions of disgust, unconsciously mimicking them in his own face and body at any threatened contact with an untouchable. Given the child's propensity to place himself at the centre of all experience, he effortlessly links the family's disapproval and revulsion toward the untouchable to those times when he has been an 'untouchable' himself, that is, the times when he has been the subject of unruly tantrums, uncontrollable urges relating to food and, above all, when he has been filthily, gloriously dirty.

All young children, everywhere in the world, try to disown their 'bad', socially disapproved dirtiness by projecting it outside. It is first projected on to animals and later to other people and groups of people—'reservoirs', as the psychoanalyst Vamik Volkan calls them.[7] These reservoirs are available to the child as a pre-selection by his own caste group. Since ages, the untouchables have been the selected reservoir of dirtiness for the upper-caste child, just as Muslims were and still are for Hindus (and vice versa). It is significant that Gandhi recollects his mother telling him when he was a child that the shortest cut to purification after touching an untouchable was to cancel the touch by an even dirtier one—by touching a Muslim.[8]

Viewing an antagonistic group as dirty, and thus subhuman, whereas one's own cleanliness is not only humanely civilized but next to godliness, is commonplace in ethnic conflict. 'Dirty nigger' and 'dirty Jew' are well-known epithets in the United States. The Chinese regard Tibetans as unwashed and perpetually stinking of yak butter, while Jewish children in Israel are brought up to regard Arabs as dirty. In the Rwandan radio broadcasts inciting the Hutus to massacre the Tutsis, the latter were consistently called rats and cockroaches, creatures associated with dirt and underground sewers, vermin that needed to be exterminated.

As the psychoanalyst Lawrence Kubie has pointed out in a classic paper, there exists in all of us, as a legacy from our early childhood, an unconscious image 'of the body as a kind of animated, mobile dirt factory exuding filth at every aperture.'[9] The disavowal of this 'dirt fantasy' can take many forms, and it is interesting to see how it operates in different cultures. There is relative unconcern in India with public hawking, belching and farting, or bringing one's hand in direct contact with faecal matter when washing one's anus (with the left hand) after defecation. In contrast, in the West there are strong taboos around bodily apertures, around noises or smells that emanate from an aperture and may draw attention to the opening and thus to the dirt factory humming behind it. The idea of spitting publicly or going to the lavatory without the protection of toilet paper will fill a Westerner with visceral disgust. Indians, on the other hand, find Western cleanliness regimens equally disgusting. There is an amusing anecdote about the well-known classical singer Siddheswari Devi of Benares who, accompanied by her daughter Pappo, went to England on a month-long concert tour. Her student and biographer, Sheila Dhar, was surprised to see her back in Benares within a week of her departure. On being asked the reason for her precipitate return, Siddheswari Devi exploded, 'Such dirty people! I will never go to Vilayat [specifically England, but a generic term for Europe] again.'

She then proceeded to elaborate:

> We were given a room upstairs in the house of a mean-faced English witch. After my journey, I naturally wanted a bath. We hardly recognized the bathroom because it had carpets on the floor! I suspected right away that these people cannot be very serious about washing themselves if they could have carpets in their bathroom. There was no brass *lota* (mug) no wooden *patta* (low seat) to sit on and scrape one's heels clean. Nothing. Just flowered carpets. Along one wall there was a long white coffin-like tub which Pappo said one could fill with water and treat like a bucket. She said she would pour the water over me with a plastic mug she found in the room. But where was I to sit? What on earth do these people do themselves, I wondered. Pappo informed me that they simply sat in the tub and splashed their own dirt on themselves and called that a bath!

Siddheswari Devi tells her daughter to roll up the carpet so that she can use the wooden boards underneath as a seat and asks her daughter to pour water over her. There are loud screams from below as the water from the singer's bath drips into their English host's fish stew.

The next morning when Siddeshwari Devi wants to use the lavatory and doesn't find a water mug, she is shocked. 'Don't they need water to clean themselves afterwards?' she asks her daughter. No, replies the daughter and shows her a roll of paper. 'This is what they use to clean themselves with.'

> I could not believe it. I asked her to swear that that was all they used, and she did. Something happened to me from that moment onwards. I felt so faint and couldn't even breathe properly...I ordered Pappo to go down and brave the witch's wrath and boldly ask for a second mug because I insist on it...the witch came bounding up the stairs to see for herself what was required...What did we want a second one for? Pappo explained as best as she could. We clean ourselves with water and our hands and the mug has to be different from the one we use for the body bath afterwards. The witch was trying to take in what Pappo was telling her but just could not believe that anyone could use their hands to clean themselves even with the aid of water. When light dawned at last, it was the witch's turn to feel faint and sick. She collapsed on a chair in shock. All I wanted was to go home as fast I could.[10]

In India, this 'dirty fantasy' is generally dealt with by projecting the unconscious image of the mobile dirt factory, of the wild animal rutting in the squalor of its own excrement, onto a group of 'outsiders': the untouchables. The brahmin can only be pure because the dalit is polluted.[11] A pure body must not come in contact with impure substances; the pure avoid impure foods such as (in large parts of the country) meat, impure professions and activities such as those of the cobbler and sweeper, and even contact with people who are looked down upon as impure.

Whereas in the West there is much effort expended in masking the dirty *inside*, in India it is directed towards shifting the dirt *outside*. We see the reflection of this psychological predilection in the immaculate cleanliness inside Indian homes and the garbage dumped outside into public spaces. As has been perceptively remarked by many before us, Indians are a very clean people who live in a filthy country.

The animated family discussions around bowel movements (pushing the faeces outside) before the start of the day have struck many Western observers of the Indian scene as obsessive. The Indian preoccupation, though, is not with faeces alone but a whole chain of substances in which faeces is only the last link. In Freudian terms (and in the words of the psychoanalyst Donald Winnicott), what is operating here, in the Indian mind, is a basic 'oral fantasy' that goes something like this: 'When hungry I think of food, when I eat I think of taking food in. I think of what I like to keep inside and I think of what I want to be rid of and I think of getting rid of it.'[12] The primary elements contributing to a dirty inside are the consumption of 'dirty' food and the retention of the 'dirty' part—'what I want to be rid of'—in the transformations of food, that is, faeces. (We will come back to the traditional ideology of food and what constitutes bad or 'dirty' food—food that lowers human consciousness—in the chapter on health.) It is no wonder that the largest set of prohibitions in interactions between castes have to do with food, and the first thing any caste attempting to raise its status does is to publicly announce a change in its food habits.

In large part, then, the equation of untouchables with dirt has to do with their consumption of 'dirty' foods, including the leftovers of higher castes that have been polluted by spittle, another product of the dirt factory that is the body. Accepting food or water from an untouchable was—and among many Indians, still remains—the surest way of losing one's caste status. For centuries, the preferred story used by Hindu reformers fighting the evil of untouchability is of the god-king Rama accepting berries from the hands of an untouchable tribal woman, Shabari.

Since the presence of faeces in the body is the second major definer of a dirty inside, there is a powerful psychological association between untouchability and faeces even when the taboo around body openings does not exist in India as in the West. The link is corroborated in the outer world by the fact that some untouchable castes have been traditional sweepers of latrines, carrying buckets of night soil on their heads.

A relatively neglected aspect of the psychological sources of untouchability is the visual aspect of dirt, its darkness as compared to the light hue of cleanliness. In the universal 'dirt fantasy', dark is dirtier (and more sinister) than fair. Generally speaking, a brahmin will be fairer than the untouchable who will tend to have the darkest complexion among all the castes. The equation of dirt with dark colour is well known to any upper-caste Indian child, especially a girl, who has been told by her mother to rub her skin every day with a mixture of dough and cream and who is convinced that the thin dark slivers sloughing off her face or arms are concrete proof of her skin becoming lighter.

Evidence of the pan-Indian preference for fair skin and a denigration bordering on scorn for the dark-skinned is all around us. Whereas in the West anti-wrinkle creams and other products against ageing are a gold mine for pharmaceutical companies, in India, especially among the middle class, products that promise a whitening of the skin chalk up record profits. Television commercials for 'Fair and Lovely' cream for women and, more recently, 'Fair and Handsome' for men; the natural equation of light skin with nobility, beauty and high birth in proverbs, tales and legends; matrimonials in newspapers and on Internet websites specifying 'fair' brides—all these are accepted as being in the natural order of things. 'Black is beautiful!' is not a slogan that will catch on in India anytime in the near future. Fair skin, then, is eminently touchable, desirable, whereas dark skin is an outer manifestation of inner dirtiness and remains 'untouchable'.

This brings us to the case of the fair-skinned foreigner and the ambivalence with which he is often regarded. On the one hand, he is a consumer of dirty, forbidden foods, especially beef, which pushes him towards the untouchable spectrum in the caste hierarchy. And, indeed, as we shall see in the chapter on health, very traditional brahmin households will still not let a foreigner enter or even come anywhere near their kitchen. On the other hand, the fair skin of the foreigner negates the presumption of dirt and untouchability. The psychological association of fair skin with everything 'clean', 'regal' and 'desirable', together with memories of being ruled by fair-skinned invaders and the presumption of wealth associated with fair-skinned visitors, makes most Indians fawn over the goras ('whites'). A dark-skinned African, on the other hand, will often be an object of condescension, even ridicule. Little wonder that many a gora leading an anonymous, run-of-the-mill life in his own country feels like a special 'somebody' in India, the admiring gazes and flattering tones of voice constantly feeding his self-esteem, his narcissism.

Coming back to the connection between the 'dirty' (and necessarily 'dark') and discrimination, we will end this section with a story. Tales and legends play a crucial role in introducing a child to his society, and the tale of the crow and the sparrow, told in many regions of India with but slight variations, conveys the culture's view of untouchability to the growing child in a narrative rather than a discursive form. In his book *Two Tales of Crow and Sparrow*, Alan Dundes relates a version of the tale from the state of Maharashtra.[13]

There was a crow who wanted to eat a sparrow's nestlings.
He once went to her house and asked for the desired feast.

The sparrow was shrewd and knew that she was unable to give an open fight to her stronger opponent. She thought for a while and said meekly to the crow, 'Oh crow! You can surely eat my babies if you want. But there is one condition. You know that you are a mahar, an untouchable, and I am a brahmin, so please do not touch my babies as you are. You must wash yourself, beak and all, and then eat them up.'

'So be it,' said the crow and went to the river. As he was about to take a dip in the water, the river said, 'Oh crow, you are a mahar, so do not enter my water.'

'Oh river, I have to bathe in the river and then go and eat the sparrow's nestlings.'

'In that case, bring a pot and take water in it.'

The crow then went to a potter and said, 'Oh potter, give me a pot. With the pot I bring water. With the water I bathe. After bathing I eat the sparrow's nestlings.'

'In that case,' said the potter, 'you have to get me earth; because all the pots that are here are broken.'

The crow then went to the earth and started digging the earth with his beak and he was not able to do much digging. So he went to the deer and begged for its horn. The deer said that if the crow could arrange a fight with a dog, then only would its horn be broken. The crow went to a dog and begged him to fight with the deer and thus help him get the horn, so that he could dig the earth and thus get a pot made by the potter and then having washed himself, he could feast on the sparrow's nestlings. The dog consented to fight but said, 'Oh crow! I need an iron ball to throw at the deer. So get it for me.' The crow then went to the ironsmith and begged for the ball. The smith made a ball in the fire and gave it to the crow. The crow held the hot burning ball in his beak and was burnt to death. The sparrow was thus spared her young ones.

To a child listening to the tale, the message on the nature of the untouchable is clear. The (untouchable) crow is black, and has a beak that forages in symbolic equivalents of faeces, refuse and garbage. (A crow is also inauspicious in the sense that in the popular mind it is a bird associated with death[14]—to dream of a crow is a sign of approaching death—and this may well be included in some versions of the story.) Naturally, then, for its presumption of going to dine on the upper-caste sparrow, the crow is fittingly punished.

These are some of the essentials of untouchability that enter into the cultural part of the growing child's mind as an underlying 'truth' of the social world in which he will live and die.

Caste, or rather what has been called 'the evil of the caste system', has been under persistent attack by Hindu reformers—chief among them, Mahatma Gandhi—for more than a century. In fact, what is now considered news is not that someone attacks the institution of caste but that someone dares to publicly defend it. The reformist attack on the religious and moral foundations of caste and the onslaught of the state on its legal pretensions has certainly weakened the hold of certain aspects of caste on the mind at least of middle-class urban Indians. The well-known sociologist André Béteille attests to this change when he writes: 'The doctor in his office, the lawyer in his chambers, the civil servant or even the clerk in his office is no longer bound by the moral authority of his caste or sub-caste in the way in which the brahmin, the rajput, the *nai* (barber) or the *dhobi* (washerman) was in the traditional village. The emancipation of the individual from the demands of the caste and sub-caste has been a complex and long-drawn process that is by no means complete yet...What is clear, however, is that increasing numbers of professionals, civil servants, managers and others feel free to repudiate such moral claims as may be made on them in the name of the caste to which they happen to belong...it is in this sense that the middle-class Indian's orientations to caste and to his family are quite different. He cannot repudiate his obligations to his family even when he finds them irksome; nothing is easier for him than to repudiate the demands of his caste if he finds them inconvenient.'[15]

Yet, even for the urban middle-class Indian there are some demands of his caste identity that lie under the surface of consciousness and thus are less susceptible to conscious examination and eventual repudiation. The occupation prescribed for his caste is the most easily rejected; what middle-class parents are most passionate about is their children's admission to those schools, colleges and professional institutions that are perceived as gateways to successful careers in the modern economy. Caste also now plays a decreasing role in middle-class friendships, and inter-caste marriages, though still rare, have begun to register on the Indian mental screen. But the hierarchical thinking associated with caste continues to remain influential in the middle-class psyche. As does the specific fantasy that associates the untouchable with the dark consumer of dirty foods.

# INDIAN WOMEN:
## TRADITIONAL AND MODERN

$\mathcal{I}$ndia was and continues to be a patriarchal society, with the general subordination of women and their disempowerment that patriarchy normally entails. To view Indian women solely through the lens of patriarchy, therefore, is to see the resemblance—in fact only superficial—to women in other patriarchal societies. But the image in such a case is always fuzzy and indistinct. Once we use the zoom lens of Indic culture (and its contemporary ferment), however, the picture becomes more focussed and nuanced as unexpected details emerge. The similarities to women in other patriarchal societies do not disappear but become balanced, and, in parts of the picture, overwhelmed by the differences. Thus, for example, in India, caste almost always trumps gender in the sense that a brahmin woman will have higher status than a low-caste man.[1] Or, to take another example, the powerful role played by mother-goddesses in the Indian cultural imagination—and by mothers in the inner worlds of their sons—imbues male dominance with the emotional colours of fear, awe, longing, surrender, and so on.

The interplay of universal patriarchal values, Indic culture and historical change in the wake of India's encounter with the

West is most clearly seen in the case of the modern, urban Indian woman. The emergence of a sizeable middle class in the last few decades, pan-Indian in character, though overwhelmingly urban, is widely regarded—with optimism by the 'modernizers' and disdain by the 'traditionalists'—as the most important development in the ongoing transformation of Indian society. Not that this middle class is exactly the same all over the country, especially in the context of women. In the South, for instance, wives participate more in their husband's lives than in the North. But overall, the similarities between middle-class men and women across the country are greater than the differences based on caste, language or region. And within this expanding middle class, it is the woman who is at the centre of changes taking place in contemporary Indian society.

Caught in the cross-fire of ideologies that seek to defend the traditional vision of Indian womanhood and those that seek to free her from the inequities of religiously sanctioned patriarchies, the modern Indian woman is engaged in a struggle between two opposing forces in her psyche as she seeks to reconcile traditional ideals with modern aspirations. To her strident critics from either the far left or right of the political spectrum she may well answer with these lines by the German poet Goethe:

> Your spirit only seeks a single quest
> So never learns to know its brother
> Two souls, alas, dwell in my breast
> And one would gladly sunder from the other.

### A DAUGHTER IS BORN

To appreciate the magnitude of change that has taken place in the psyche of the educated, middle-class Indian woman, let us consider the culture's marked preference for a son, a preference which has scarred the psyche of generations of women.

The inner experience of being a girl, to sense that perhaps with your birth you have brought less joy to those you love, to feel that sinking of the heart when adult eyes glow at the sight of your baby brother while they dim as they regard you, can easily become a fundamental crisis at the beginning of a little girl's identity development. The crisis, generally silent, is given rare eloquent voice in the fictionalized reminiscences of the Hindi writer Mrinal Pande who describes the reactions of her fictional counterpart, the seven-year-old Tinu, at the birth of a brother after three daughters have been born to the parents.

An aunt comes in with a gleaming bowl of special broth for Mother that smells of fennel and coriander and ghee. Little slivers of chopped almonds and pistachios swim on the surface like tiny sail-boats. Mother smiles and says she doesn't feel like drinking the heavy stuff. 'Drink it up, drink it all up,' says Grandmother coming into the room and bending to pick up my younger sister. 'You will be breast-feeding a son this time.' Mother elevates herself on one elbow. I nudge against her so some of the vile liquid spills. I expect to be yelled at, to have my shoulder firmly grabbed and be propelled out of the room for bad behaviour. But nothing of that sort happens. People can't stop smiling with pleasure today.

'This is my Laxmi [goddess of good luck] daughter,' says Grandmother, squeezing my baby sister against her ample breasts. 'She has brought a brother on her back.' Everyone smiles some more...

'You too have a brother now,' everyone tells us happily. 'He'll protect you and carry on your father's name.'

Dinu [her sister] and I giggle at the thought of the little bundle protecting us. The elders' joy is infectious...

'I'm glad it's all over now,' mother tells her mother. 'No more ordeals like this for me,' she says, and lies down, content as a cat.

    'Shoo now,' Grandmother says to us, not unkindly, 'let your mother rest.'

    We are almost at the door when mother asks us anxiously if we have eaten. Her eyes are brown and deep and they are saying, Never mind. I'll love you all the same. Dinu and I smile and speak together: 'Yes we have.'

    Though the truth is, we have not.[2]

The preference for sons is as old as Indian society itself. Vedic verses pray that sons will be followed by still more male offspring, never by females. A prayer in the Atharva Veda even adds a touch of malice: 'The birth of a girl, grant it elsewhere, here grant a son.' As the Indologist A.A. MacDonnel observes, 'Indeed daughters are conspicuous in the Rig Veda by their absence. We meet in hymns with prayers for sons and grandsons, male offspring, male descendants and male issue and occasionally for wives but never daughters. Even forgiveness is asked for ourselves and grandsons, but no blessing is ever prayed for a daughter.'[3]

At the birth of a son drums are beaten in some parts of the country, conch-shells blown in others and the midwife paid lavishly, while no such spontaneous rejoicing accompanies the birth of a daughter. Women's folk songs reveal the painful awareness of this discrepancy, at birth, between the celebration of sons and the mere tolerance of daughters. Thus, in a North Indian song the women complain:

> Listen O Sukhma, what a tradition has started!
> Drums are played upon the birth of a boy,
> But at my birth only a brass plate was beaten.

And in Maharashtra, the girl, comparing herself to a white sweet-scented jasmine (*jai*) and the boy to a big, strong-smelling thorny leaf (*kevada*) plaintively asks: 'Did anyone notice the sweet fragrance of a jai? The hefty kevada however has filled the whole street with its strong scent.' A contemporary proverb from Bengal at the opposite end of the country expresses the culturally sanctioned preference more bluntly: 'Even the piss of a son brings money; let the daughter go to hell.'

Of course, the preference for the birth of a son although widespread is not uniform. But the exceptions generally only prove the rule: in some families, the first-born girl, though not as welcome as a son, may still be regarded by parents as a harbinger of good luck, or the birth of a girl after a succession of sons in a daughterless family will almost certainly be celebrated (the birth of a second or third daughter, however, tends to be an unhappy event for the family). Only in parts of the country—the North East and the south-western states— which have a history of matrilineal systems of female inheritance and post-marriage residence in the woman's house is the birth of a girl a consistently welcome event. But even these patterns are rapidly changing in the direction of the ones prevailing in the rest of the country.

Besides the universal patriarchal preoccupation with the family name being carried forward through the male line, there are ritual and economic reasons for the strong preference for male offspring. The presence of a son is necessary for the proper performance of many sacraments among the Hindus, especially those carried out following the death of parents for the well-being of their souls. Economically, a daughter is looked upon as an unmitigated expense, someone who will never contribute to the family income and who, upon marriage, will take away a considerable part of her family's fortune as her dowry. In case of a poor family, the parents may be pushed deep into debt in order to provide for a daughter's marriage. The *Aitareya Brahmana* (like other ancient texts) probably refers as much as anything else to the economic facts of life when it states flatly that a daughter is a source of misery while a son is the saviour of the family.

As the wildly skewed sex-ratios in Punjab, Haryana and Delhi, hinting at widespread female foeticide, show, economic prosperity and the rise of a sizeable middle class in these North Indian states have failed to dent the traditional preference for a son. What is encouraging, though, are signs that whatever their initial disappointment after the birth of a daughter, parents in middle-class families may have begun to take equal pleasure in their male and female offspring, at least as long as they are infants.[4] In their interactions with the baby, they do not show a preference for boys over girls, irrespective of whether they are engaging with the baby through caregiving activities or through play. The discrimination, when it takes place, begins later.

### DISCRIMINATION AND THE MAIDEN

As she grows up, the girl child sees the preference for a son translated into a differential treatment received by girls in the family. In Mrinal Pande's fictionalized reminiscences, on a visit to her maternal grandmother who lives with her son's family, the four-year-old Tinu is immediately aware of the difference between her and her male cousin Anu who is of the same age. Whether it is in the making of coloured paper buntings for a wedding where Anu takes the best twigs, leaving rotten, damp ones for Tinu and her sister, or the small peacock made of gold thread which the sisters discover but are forced to cede to their cousin under intense pressure from the adults, including their own mother, it is evident to little Tinu that as the son's son Anu cannot imagine anyone refusing him anything for long.

On a visit to the parental home of her *mami* (mother's brother's wife), Tinu listens to her mami's father muttering, 'Too many girls! Too many girls in all the nice houses!' as he feeds a slice of mango or a toffee to one of his grandsons. Back in Tinu's own family, if there are any complaints from the tutor about the girls' lack of concentration, the older women smile and say something about girls eventually needing skills only to roll chapattis and boil dal and rice. The grandmother's old female servant, while locking up the family's pet bitch for the night, says this is how she wants all girls to be: behind closed gates and asleep after dark. Even Tinu's mother is not completely immune from the traditional ideology in relation to the girl child: 'When Dinu and I laugh too much, Mother gets angry and says we will now weep. Girls should not laugh too much, she says grumpily. Dinu and I giggle inside our quilts, and then we put pretend-tears on our cheeks with our spit to ward off bad luck.'[5]

The traditional discrimination against the girl child is reflected in various statistics of which the worst is her *absence*, by the millions, in the latest census figures. Together with untouchability, the selective abortion of the female foetus and female infanticide, often by the midwife, who is paid by the family to snuff out the life of a baby girl at birth, are perhaps the greatest blots of shame on Indian society. Statistics tell us that there is a higher rate of female infant mortality; girl infants are breast-fed less frequently, for shorter durations and over shorter periods than boys; they are given lower quality food, made to work longer hours than boys and have lesser access to schooling and health care.[6]

These, then, are the objective facts of discrimination against daughters in traditional India. But what is the subjective reality? How is a factual discrimination viewed by the girls themselves? We know that what is psychologically significant is not what has happened to us but what we *believe* occurred. The fictions we tell ourselves about our past and our lives are indispensable to keep at bay the truth that may shock us out of our ever-precarious sense of well-being and self-worth. A comprehensive study of the girl child, resulting from a survey conducted among girls between the ages of seven and eighteen in six hundred rural and urban households in eight Indian states, reminds us of the gulf that often exists between objective facts and their subjective perception.[7] If the question is raised whether an Indian girl *feels* discriminated against and treated unfairly in relation to her brother, then the answer is not as clear-cut as in little Tinu's account, or as the statistics would have us believe. In the *conscious* perception of Indian girls, cutting across income, educational and regional divides, the answer to the question of gender-based discrimination is in fact more no than yes. In the study, the girls do not report differences between girls and boys with respect to health care or food (even if girls often eat last, with their mothers). Girls do not discern differences in rewards and punishments meted out to boys and girls. And as far as education is concerned, over seventy per cent of the girls—with the percentage becoming much higher in the states of Kerala and Maharashtra—believe the acquisition of literacy equally important for both boys and girls.

The main reason for the subjective perception of girls diverging from objective realities is that the cultural preference for sons and the discrimination against daughters captured in statistics (or in a creative writer's easier access to buried childhood memories) does not directly impinge upon the psyche of an Indian girl. The patriarchal stance towards the girl child is mediated and strained through the filter of the family. In other words, for the wider culture's devaluation of women to be translated into a pervasive sense of worthlessness or bitterness in individual women, the behaviour and attitudes of parents and close older relatives towards the infant girls in their midst—the actualities of family life, that is—must be fully consistent with this female depreciation. In the childhood memoirs of many women there is often one or more caretaker— an older relative—whose attitude towards and interactions with the little girl run contrary to the dictates of patriarchy.

Also, the internalization of low self-esteem presupposes that girls and women in Indian households have no sphere of their own. That they have no independent livelihood and activity, no area of family and community responsibility and control. That they have no living space, apart from that of men, within which to manifest those aspects of feminine identity that derive from intimacy and collaboration with other women. The fact, however, is that all these circumstances do exist in traditional India, mitigating the discriminations and inequities of patriarchal attitudes and institutions.

From anthropological accounts and other sources, we know of the affection and often compassionate attention bestowed by mothers on their daughters throughout their lives.[8] 'I turn the stone flour mill with the swiftness of a running deer; that is because my arms are strong with the mother's milk I drank.' This and other similar couplets sung by women all over India bear witness to the daughter's memory of her mother's affection for her and to the self-esteem and strength of will this has generated in turn.

In addition to her mother's empathic connection with her, as an Indian girl grows up, her relationships with others within the extended family contain the possibility of diluting the resentment she may harbour against her brothers. Among the many adults who comprise the joint family there is usually one adult who gives a little girl the kind of admiration and the sense of being singled out as special that a male child more often receives. And of course when a girl is the *only* daughter, such chances are increased immeasurably. Thus in folk tales, however many sons a couple may have, there is often one daughter in their midst who is the parents' favourite.

In Tinu's case, besides the gift of a rich inner life and the resources of a poetic imagination, it is her emotional access to her father that enables her to deal with the discrimination in a creative way without becoming embittered.

If no one is going to pay attention to me, then I want to be able to float free, grubby and uncombed in the large, lonely and bare rooms where I can dance with shadows after Dinu and Mother have taken off for Grandmother's crowded and noisy house...

I love being left behind.

Once they have turned the corner, I rush in, knowing that now the house will be all mine. Now I can sing, I can laugh, I can pull faces in the mirror, and dig for worms in the garden. I can also have Father all to myself when he comes home for lunch. I can spin tales to entertain him while he is eating, and he will nod good-naturedly, overlooking the spills I cause in my excitement.

But it is not easy to be left behind...⁹

In traditional India, every female is born into a well-defined community of women within her particular family. Although by no means does it resound with solidarity and goodwill, the existence of this exclusive sphere of femininity and domesticity gives a woman a tangible opportunity to be productive and lively. Getting along with other women in this sphere, learning the mandatory skills of householding, cooking and childcare, establishing her place in this primary world—these relationships and tasks constitute the dailiness of traditional girlhood in India. Moreover, when necessary, other women in the family— her mother, aunts, sisters, sisters-in-law—are not only an Indian girl's teachers and models but her allies against the discriminations and inequities of the patriarchal values of the outside world. Often enough, in the 'underground' of female culture, as reflected in ballads, wedding songs and jokes, women do indeed react against the discrimination of their wider culture by portraying men as vain, faithless and infantile.¹⁰ 'Do not call a snake "helpless", or a husband "mine",' lament the women in Maharashtra; 'A husband so long as he is in bed, Yama [god of death] when he gets up,' say Telugu wives; and women in Karnataka mock, 'Peacock before marriage, a lion at the time of engagement and a sheep after marriage.'

And finally, the young girl has before her the examples of older women, mothers all, who are respected and powerful in family affairs. The much-maligned Hindu law giver Manu is only a qualified misogynist. His infamous pronouncements against women are limited to *younger* women: 'The teacher is ten times more venerable than the sub-teacher, the father a hundred times more than the teacher, but the mother is a thousand times more than the father.'[11]

All these factors help to mitigate the damage done to a girl's self-esteem when she discovers that in the eyes of her culture and society she is considered inferior to a boy.

Leaving aside the objective facts of discrimination against daughters in middle-class families, which are almost certainly less than in traditional India, subjectively many of these girls are convinced that their parents consider them as equal to their brothers. In fact, standing the gender discrimination paradigm on its head is a study of one hundred and thirty school boys and ninety school girls from the city of Pune which reports that girls perceive themselves to be *more* accepted by both parents than do boys.[12] And what does one make of another study that tells us that educated middle-class Indian women report both parents as more 'caring', that is, affectionate, empathic and close, than do comparable women in the United States?[13] In short, as a middle-class girl grows up, her experience of gender-based discrimination in her family is substantially less than the developmental fate of her traditional counterpart.

The difference between the urban middle-class girl and the traditional rural girl is most pronounced in the area of education. For although the idea of some school education for girls has gained wide acceptance all over the country, middle-class parents even welcome *higher* education for their daughters which, they believe, is necessary for the girl so that she can achieve a measure of autonomy. University education will enable the daughter to contribute to the family income after marriage and also make her capable of standing on her own feet if, unfortunately, the marriage breaks up, a possibility that has recently dawned on the middle-class horizon.[14] The daughter is thus encouraged to work hard at her studies, her academic achievements greeted with parental pride and pleasure, while her involvement in domestic chores, although still more than that of her brother, is often minor as compared to the lot of her rural sister.

## ENTERING PUBERTY

Late childhood marks the beginning of an Indian girl's deliberate training in how to be a good woman, and hence the conscious inculcation of culturally designated feminine roles. This is true of all girls, although in the new middle class the break between early and late childhood is not so sharp and traditional feminine values are leavened with modern imports.

Like her traditional counterpart, the middle-class Indian girl entering puberty learns that the 'virtues' of womanhood which will take her through life are submission and docility in the home of her husband, and that the primary goal of her life is to please her future husband and parents-in-law. This learning, however, is now being subverted by a middle-class modernity that is pushing the girl toward educational achievement, equality and relative independence. The message from her parents is mixed. Obedience and conformity, selflessness and self-denial are still the ideals of womanhood and a good woman does not 'create waves' or 'rock the boat'. Middle-class parents, however, also encourage and take pride in the academic success of their daughter. Their aspirations for an occupational career for her, though more ambiguous than for a son, are not completely absent. The parents' cherished goal for the daughter, however, remains a 'good' marriage; her education should help the girl to find a well-educated, economically well-off man from a respectable family. Which is not to say that this is always the case. But if a girl pursues education solely and determinedly for a career, it is usually when a strong and self-reliant adult member of her immediate family has empowered her through approval or encouragement. Clinical experience and group discussions with middle-class women suggest that in families where mothers are not career women, a daughter looks up to and identifies with the father as the representative of the modern, external world. *His* is the decisive voice in influencing her career choice and legitimizing her intellectual aspirations.

The faltering in self-esteem of Indian girls during the years of early puberty is intimately related to the fact that at precisely this developmental moment, a time of hormonal changes and emotional volatility, her training in service and self-denial in preparation for her imminent roles of daughter-in-law and wife is stepped up. In order to maintain her family's love and approval—the narcissistic supplies necessary for firm self-esteem—the girl tends to conform, and even over-conform, to the prescriptions and expectations of those around her.

Puberty is also the period when the differential treatment of girls cannot be masked. Besides the training to be a good wife and daughter-in-law, a major difference in the bringing up of sons and daughters is in the restrictions placed on the girl's freedom of movement. Whether strictly enforced or relatively lenient, the restrictions transcend rural–urban, traditional–modern and other demographic differences. In traditional India, girls are not allowed to play with boys and are confined to the company of their own sex. There are many prohibitions with regard to the kind of clothes they may wear. A girl is permitted fewer recreational activities which involve going out of the house such as visiting friends, going to the market or to the cinema, and which may bring her in contact with a member of the opposite sex.

Puberty rites in many parts of the country emphasize the fact of the girl's body 'flowering' or 'ripening' into womanhood and thus being ready to fulfil what the culture regards as the chief tasks of a woman's life cycle—procreation and motherhood. The girl's sexual maturity is welcomed as a vital step on the road to becoming a woman whose fertility would be a credit to the family. Yet, the same puberty is also feared because of the inherent danger of wantonness and sexual abandon which can deeply dishonour and shame her family and the community. The girl has to be protected—from herself as much from men—in the highly vulnerable period between puberty and marriage, a period to be kept as short as possible. This protection mainly translates itself into the culture's efforts at moulding the ways the girl carries herself and in placing restrictions on her encounters with men. For instance, it is expected from the girl that she never take long 'masculine' strides but short, soft, barely audible steps, which are also forced upon her by the sari or the half sari she now has to wear. Traditionally, all actions that could even hint at sexual abandon—personified by the prostitute, the dancing-girl or the courtesan—such as the bold gaze or the loud laugh, the chewing of betel leaf (*paan*) which tints the mouth red, leaning against a pillar or wall or standing in the doorway meet with undisguised family disapproval.[15]

This applies more now to rural and small-town communities in India. The restrictions placed on the way an urban middle-class girl comports herself are more relaxed. But they are by no means absent. The average college girl in Delhi, for instance, dressed in jeans or even short skirts, will perhaps smile at the antics of a boy playing the clown to attract her attention but will hesitate to break into loud laughter. At some level, she is still aware of traditional folk 'wisdom' pertaining to male-female interactions in this period of her life which she has absorbed from the family and community in the process of growing up and which, for instance, holds that boys believe '*Jo hansi, woh phansi*' ('If a girl laughs, she is already in the net').

The restrictions, enforced by the women of the family, by mothers and grandmothers, are not presented to the girl as punitive measures but as the reality of the world in which she will live. The curbs on her freedom are the way things 'naturally' are, and to which the girl, any 'good girl', must comply for her own protection and the good name of the family. The message transmitted to the girl is that it is *she* who is responsible for maintaining a distance from boys and men, thereby protecting her 'purity' which is also the honour (*izzat*) of the whole family. She is made to understand, undermining a sense of female agency, that young women are weak and vulnerable, unable to resist determined male advances or the promptings of their own sexual nature.

Even middle-class girls are not overly rebellious or critical of the restrictions on their free association with boys. Although overwhelmingly in favour of co-education, the majority of college girls, at least in small towns and cities, would like their interaction with boys to be limited to educational activities and not extend to a more personal association, and certainly not to 'dating' in the Western sense.

Within this atmosphere of general avoidance of close contact with men, there is one poignant fact: the little time a daughter spends with her father. In traditional India, less than half the families (almost two-thirds in Bihar, Orissa and Uttar Pradesh) eat together at meal time, almost the only time a girl may have with her father. Although the contact between father and daughter is greater in urban, middle-class families, it is still generally limited. The absent father, without a share in the activities of his daughter, indeed 'reflects one of the great tragedies of Indian family life.'[16]

We do not mean to over-emphasize the bleakness of puberty in the life cycle of a traditional Indian girl. One compensation of this period is an increase in culturally sanctioned maternal indulgence, paradoxically at the same time when the mother is also the chief agent in the family's efforts in moulding the girl according to the dictates of tradition. Considered as a guest in her 'natal' family, the girl is often treated with the solicitous concern accorded to a welcome outsider who, all too soon, will marry and leave her mother for good. Mindful of her daughter's fate, the mother re-experiences the emotional conflicts her own separation once aroused, and this in turn tends to increase her indulgence and solicitude toward her daughter. As we have noted above, daughterhood in India is not without its rewards precisely because the conditions of young womanhood are normally so forbidding. Little wonder that for an Indian girl rebellion against the constraints of impinging womanhood, with all its circumscription of identity, becomes near impossible. She internalizes the specific ideals of womanhood and monitors her behaviour carefully in order to guarantee her mother's love and approval, upon which she is more than ever dependent as she makes ready to leave home. The irony of an Indian girl's coming of age is that to be a good woman and a felicitous bride she must be more than ever the perfect daughter.

## MARRIAGE: IS LOVE NECESSARY?

In traditional India, the marriage of a daughter is a trying time for the whole family and often overwhelming for the young girl. Consider this: in northern India, given the rules that a marriage should be within the same caste or a group of sub-castes but exclude partners from the extended kinship group (which practically eliminates all eligible males of the village), it is likely that a girl will marry a stranger from a place far away from the one in which she has spent her childhood. More important, she may have little say in the choice of her partner, and this is a pan-Indian phenomenon.

As we shall see later, modern Indian girls also prefer arranged marriages, though their sense of their own agency in the arranging of the marriage is greater. Whereas considerations of caste and family status, followed by the earning power of the boy are dominant in the arrangement of traditional marriages, education and the 'personality' of the groom— apart, of course, from the social and monetary status of the groom's family—are now the more important considerations for the new middle class. And it is in this class that the girl's opinion is not only sought but actively solicited. Often enough, she has a de facto power of veto on any marriage alliance proposed on her behalf. Paradoxically, because of the spread of the global consumer culture in which the Indian middle class is an enthusiastic participant, the amount of cash and material goods expected as dowry by the groom are today far greater than the more modest expectation of giving and taking in traditional Hindu marriages.

In spite of her inner ideals and conscious resolutions to be a good wife and an exemplary daughter-in-law, a bride comes into her husband's family with heightened anxiety and feelings of loss. There is a wariness bordering on antagonism toward her mother-in-law who has usurped the place of her own sorely missed and needed mother. There is a mixture of shy anticipation and resentment towards her husband's sisters and young female relatives who are presuming to replace the sisters and cousins and friends at home. And then there are the ambivalent feelings of hope and fear towards the usually unknown man who is now her husband and claims her intimacy.

Further, in the social hierarchy of her new family, the bride normally occupies a low rank. Obedience and compliance with the wishes of the mother-in-law are expected as a matter of course. Any mistakes or omissions on her part are liable to incur sarcastic references to her abilities, her looks or her upbringing in her mother's home. The bride's situation is not quite so bad in middle-class marriages. Marrying late, typically in her early twenties, the middle-class woman no longer enters her husband's family as a submissive daughter-in-law. Because of her education and maturity, she begins to play a significant role in her husband's family affairs from the very outset. The middle-class woman's potential for individual self-assertion in her marriage and the new family has, however, clearly defined limits which come from her traditional 'markings', etched deep into her mind during the process of growing up. She, too, believes that getting along in her husband's family and earning the good opinion of his family members, including the traditionally reviled and feared mother-in-law, are important obligations—even when these entail a measure of self-sacrifice and self-denial.

Here, it helps that an Indian girl is prepared or at least sufficiently warned about what to expect before she actually departs for her husband's home. Guidance by the mother and other female relatives on what awaits her in her new home— stories, proverbs, songs, information gleaned from newly married friends who come back home on visits—have more or less prepared her for the harshness of the transition. If married very young, the bride's initiation into her new life is gradual, interspersed by visits to her parents' home where much of her accumulated loneliness and resentment can be relieved by the indulgent love showered on her. Even in the husband's home, the young wife's isolation is relieved by relationships of informal familiarity that she might form with certain younger members of the new family, and especially with other fellow-sufferers— the daughters-in-law of the house.

We need to add that although the clichéd relationship between an overweening mother-in-law and a silently suffering daughter-in-law is a bitter reality for many young women, the changes that are taking place in the power structure of the educated middle class have made many a mother-in-law view herself as a loser across the board. She feels bitter and shortchanged that although she suffered under the whims and moods of older family members when she was a young bride, now, when it is her turn to reap the fruits of being the family matriarch, she can neither take the respect of her better educated daughter-in-law or the loyalty of her son for granted.

Although the cruel mother-in-law and the suffering daughter-in-law (including the eventual triumph of the younger woman over her older antagonist) is the staple of many women's songs, folk tales and of widely watched TV soaps, it is rarely recognized that the reviled mother-in-law is but an agent of the Indian family. Given the organizing principle of the traditional Indian family, in which the parent–son and filial bonds are more central than the husband–wife tie (that is considered the fulcrum of the modern Western family), the new bride constitutes a very real threat to the unity of the larger family. Abundantly aware of the power of sex to overthrow religiously sanctioned family values and long established social norms, the family is concerned that the young wife may cause her husband to neglect his duties as a son, as a brother, a nephew, an uncle; that he will transfer his loyalty and affection to her rather than remaining truly a son of the house.

These are not either/or choices; however, custom, tradition and the interests of the family demand that in the realignment of roles and relationships initiated by the son's marriage, the couple not take centre stage, at least not in the early years of marriage. Signs of developing attachment and tenderness between husband and wife are carefully monitored and their development discouraged. Oblique hints about 'youthful infatuation', or outright shaming virtually guarantee that the young husband and wife do not publicly express affection for each other; and they are effectively alone together only for very brief periods during the night. The much-maligned mother-in-law, besides (or even because of) being animated by her own possessiveness in relation to her son, is no more than the family's designated agent preventing the build-up of a 'foreign' cell in the family body.

One would expect the transition of marriage to be easier for women in South India with its tradition of cross-cousin and uncle–niece marriages which ensure that women are not married to complete strangers and do not have to settle down far from their parental homes. Marriages should be even easier for women in places like Kerala with its history of matrilineal families in sections of its population. The 'higher' status of women, however, does not seem to relieve the stresses and strains of marriage for the young girl to any appreciable degree: Kerala, for instance, reports high levels of dowry-related deaths among women, while Thiruvananthapuram (Trivandrum), the state's capital, ranks among the highest in the prevalence of domestic violence in Indian cities.[17] High levels of literacy and participation in employed work, greater freedom and decision-making authority, as in the case of women in Tamil Nadu, are not enough to overthrow the weight of cultural norms governing the role and behaviour expected of a newly married woman.[18]

We have said that the commonly shared, pan-Indian notion of marriage is not of a relationship between two individuals but an alliance between two families or, more, between two clans. The choice of the partner, then, is not individual but arranged by the family. Although, as we've seen, in more modern families young people have the right of veto on their parents' choice of the partner, even here there is a subtle gender discrimination; the consultations with the daughter are often more perfunctory than those with the son.

Arranged marriages are not only a pan-Indian norm, cutting across the divides of education, social class, religion and region, they are also rarely seen as an imposition by the young people concerned, who overwhelmingly prefer them to the kind of love marriages typical of contemporary Western societies. The preference is partly based on the young person's acceptance of the cultural definition of marriage as a family rather than an individual affair, where harmony and shared values that come from a common background are more important than individual fascination.

Love marriages also have a bad press in India in the sense that they are reputed to turn out to be generally unhappy. This reputation is more than just rumour or prejudice, not because of the love between the young people that initiated the marriage but because of the social attitudes that put the marriage under enormous pressure. Thus, for instance, a study of men and women of different castes from fifteen villages in Tamil Nadu reveals that only five out of the seventy women had made marriages that were not arranged. None of the five had parental support for the wedding; they had to elope and get married in a temple. The author writes, 'All but one of the five women now regret their decision. The opposition from the husbands' parents has made their lives miserable. Their husbands have not been able to break away from their parents because of financial constraints, and the woman having come "empty-handed" [with no gold or cash as is usual in a traditional wedding], and not having any support from her natal family, has only exacerbated matters.'[19]

Perhaps the greatest attraction of an arranged marriage is the fact that it takes away the young person's anxiety around finding a mate. Whether you are plain or good-looking, fat or thin, you can be sure that a suitable mate will be found for you. Although physical beauty is important for the Indian girl, it does not command the same premium in the selection of a partner as it does in Western societies. In India, the beauty industry can certainly dip into the woman's latent desire to be beautiful, a desire which may have been pent up in traditional India for a long time and has now begun to find a voice. It cannot, however, as it does in the West, mobilize the woman's fear of never finding a mate merely because she has not done enough to enhance her looks.

The consensus in favour of arranged marriage through the centuries is truly astonishing; in fact, the only ancient Hindu text that considers the love marriage as the highest form of marriage is the revolutionary *Kamasutra*. What, then, of Bollywood movies where love marriage reigns and is depicted as the only road to happiness?[20]

Now love and the lyrical impulse of its narration are indeed universal, one of the few constants left in a world that makes a fetish of cultural relativism. Erotic passion, with love's tender discoveries, sudden torments and consuming desires, is one of the last bastions of our common humanity. Indians, too, are enamoured of the love story, of (Bollywood) tales about young lovers who are believed to express the purest of romantic sentiments. In India, as in most other cultures through history, the love story has never been a reflection but a subverter of the accepted mores prescribing the relations between the sexes.[21] The pleasure we take in this subversion is one of the many enduring fascinations of the love story which is a vehicle for the vicarious satisfaction of our hidden desires and obscure longings.

The love story, whether in movies or fiction, is the dream of capturing love's freshness and spontaneity free of all social restrictions and internal inhibitions and of becoming one with the beloved while overwhelming the forces that would dampen desire and the urge to merge. In a society that is deeply hierarchical, with caste and class barriers which are not easy to cross even by the god of love Kama, the dream is of love unimpeded by the shackles of family obligations and duties toward the old and all the other keepers of society's traditions.

Bollywood movies are thus not a guide to Indian marriage but a doorway into the universal dream of love; what they offer are not role models for the young but romantic nostalgia for the freshness of love's vision to men and women of all ages.

What happens to love in an arranged marriage? Is it fated to remain a dream, an unslaked thirst? Must it be completely submerged in the arranged marriage's ideal of safety? An arranged marriage does not quite obliterate the allure of the dream of love, although it must be admitted that it mutes the dream's vivid colours. Studies show that in the case of poor women in traditional India, the expectations from a potential husband are pretty basic: 'He should not drink or beat me, and support me and the family'.[22] Women belonging to higher strata may have additional expectations, namely that the husband be educated, have a salaried employment and be 'modern' in the sense of not unduly restricting the freedom of his wife. In the upper classes, where the expectations are even greater, young women still do not enter marriage with as high hopes as in the West. The woman does not expect, as is often the case in Western societies, that the partner will satisfy *all* her emotional needs and longings, that her husband will not only be an adult sexual man but also a father, mother, a little baby boy and a twin brother (and vice versa in the case of a man). Her demands on the husband, mostly unconscious, to fulfil these multiple roles—rather than their being spread over the larger family as in India—can certainly be a source of disquiet in Western marriages.

Yet even in India, in-depth interviews with women from the poorest slums reveal that their dream of love, of integrating tenderness with eroticism, mutual respect with caring, has not disappeared.[23] Its location, though, is not the same as in the West. Love is not looked for *before* marriage but ideally arises in the *jodi* (couple) that comes into existence *after* marriage.

The squalor of slum life does nothing to dim the luminosity

of the women's romantic longing to experience the husband's love. On the contrary, the abysmal material conditions and the struggle against poverty arouses their 'sense of life according to love'—to quote the poet Philip Larkin—to its fullest wakefulness. The dream of the transforming power of love, of what the woman might have been if she were well and truly loved, is tenaciously clung to amidst (and perhaps because of) all the suffering and pathos of her existence.

The central image of this dream is the couple or jodi. The couple, of course, exerts a universally powerful pull on the human imagination, given our deeply buried wish to be seen by the spouse as god might have done—that is, with absolute love and total understanding. It is telling that in spite of the social consensus in favour of the joint family and widespread praise of its virtues, the couple continues to remain a lodestar in the cultural imagination of Indian women. Iconically represented as the *mithuna* (sexual intercourse) couple in medieval temple sculptures, its highest manifestation is *ardhanarishwara*—the Lord who is half woman, a visualization of the jodi as a single two-person entity. This is the cultural ideal which makes a Hindu invoke a deity not on its own but as a couple: Sitarama and not Sita and Rama, Radhakrishna and not Radha and Krishna.

The persistence and importance of the jodi for the woman's sense of identity helps us comprehend better why many women, in spite of their economic independence, choose to suffer humiliation rather than leave an oppressive husband; why some women, in times of extreme marital stress and burning rage towards the spouse, exercise the option of suicide rather than separation. It is the persistence of this ideal which explains why a woman, from any class, is apt to deny the presence of marital problems, such as a husband's alcohol abuse and violence, in order to hold aloft the portrait of a happy couple. To confess to an unhappy marriage is not only to reconcile one's self to the loss of a cherished personal goal but also betray a powerful cultural ideal.

The profound yearning of a wife, as a woman, for intimacy with the husband—as a man—is an overwhelming issue in fiction and in the lives of middle-class patients seen in psychotherapy. Connecting the various stages of a woman's adulthood, from an expectant bride to a more sober grandmother, the intense wish to create a two-person universe with the husband where each finally 'recognizes' the other, is never far from her consciousness. It is a beacon of hope amidst the toil, drudgery, fights, disappointments and occasional joys of her stormy existence within the extended family. The dream of finding love in marriage is tenaciously clung to through the suffering and pathos of her existence as a young bride. This love is a quieter affair, without the delicious delirium that can mark the periods of courtship and the beginning of a marriage in the West; its feeling-tone is of contented togetherness rather than ecstasy. In other words, the dream of love remains necessary for marriage. The difference is that in Indian marriages this love has a different quality; it is less romantically or erotically imperious and does not have to prefigure marriage but can waft in gently afterwards, sometimes years later, when the couple is well into adulthood.

There are, of course, objective conditions for the likelihood of the couple falling in love after marriage. Arranged marriages work best, and perhaps *can* only work, if the sexes are kept apart in youth and if marriages are early, before young men and women have had an opportunity to compare a range of potential partners. Except for a minuscule upper class, these conditions hold substantially true for the rest of Indian society. The hormonal pressure created by enforced celibacy during youth and a lack of experience with the opposite sex ensure that the young person is biologically and emotionally primed to fall in love if the marriage partner is even reasonably satisfactory.

### THE HOME AND THE WORLD

Urban, upper-caste, educated women began working outside the home in any significant number only after the 1940s. Earlier, it would have been unthinkable for a girl from a respectable family to enter the labour market and look for work. This process of middle-class women working for pay has accelerated since the 1970s, chiefly due to two reasons: One, the change in the traditional view about the education of a daughter which now encourages higher education for girls and thus makes their participation in socially respectable work possible; and two, the growing financial needs of middle-class families, partly due to their higher consumption aspirations.

Most educated middle-class women work in lower- or middle-level white-collar jobs as clerks, secretaries, telephone operators or at better paid jobs in the mushrooming call centres. Those who are professionally qualified are found in the fields of school and college teaching, medicine and research. In the last decade, a small but significant number of middle-class women have branched out from what were long considered suitable occupations for women to enter the fields of advertising, computer software, corporate management, or to set up as small-scale entrepreneurs. Most of these women however show a much greater investment in their career than is usually the case with a majority of middle-class working women.

Women who are working or have worked for remuneration in the past, feel that as compared to their mothers, their higher education and professional qualifications have had a definite influence on increasing their social status and self-esteem. For women who continue to work, their contentment with the freedom of movement and a measure of independence provided by the job is palpable. Even the non-working middle-class woman exudes a greater self-confidence than her mother's generation. She believes she has a higher degree of control over her own destiny since her education will enable her to enter the labour market should the need ever arise. Having a job is not as important to her self-esteem as the fact that she is qualified to hold one.

As one would expect, the middle-class woman's interest in wider social, cultural and political concerns—fostered through the watching of TV, reading of magazines and, to a lesser extent, of newspapers—is much more than that of the traditional woman. On the other hand, though, the middle-class woman is lonelier than her traditional counterpart. The latter's immersion in joint family life and in well-marked sectors of domestic, social and ritual activities carried out in communities of women had absorbed her energy and fulfilled most of her needs for friendship and intimacy. The modern middle-class woman's bonds with the family—her own and that of her husband's—are weaker, her friendships intermittent and her social circle narrower. The missing intimacy in her life is increasingly demanded from, and with some luck provided by, her husband.

Tradition continues its hold on the middle-class woman's mind in that she views domestic and maternal obligations as central to her identity. This is true of the housewife as much as of the high-profile career woman. Traditional norms which demand that a woman's first commitment be to her children and the second to her husband, do not seem to be influenced by a woman's educational or occupational status. Working wives who express satisfaction with their career still rank the raising of children as the highest goal of a woman's life. Here a decided lag between the values of middle-class husbands and wives is apparent. In a fifteen-year-old study carried out in Bangalore, most wives ranked the traditional purposes of marriage—children, love and affection, fulfilment of the husband's sexual needs (rather than her own)—very high. The husbands, on the other hand, ranked the goals of a supposedly more modern marriage—comfortable life, companionship and fulfilment of individual sexual needs—higher than their wives.[24] Perhaps with the exception of upper-middle-class women, our impression is that what Indian women consciously want from marriage—as contrasted to their more subterranean wishes around the jodi—has not changed to any marked degree.

In some ways, the middle-class woman, whether she is working or not, is even more child centered than her traditional counterpart. For instance, she has taken on the primary responsibility for the education of her young children and plays a key role in arranging the children's recreational activities, areas which used to be earlier in the domain of the husband and elder male members of the joint family. The life of the non-working woman seems to be wholly organized around her children's needs, the rhythm of her day determined by their various activities. The achievements of the children, especially educational, are her biggest source of satisfaction and validation as a woman. Irrespective of whether she is working or not, the middle-class woman's maternal role is not an imposition but freely and joyfully chosen; motherhood remains the acme of a fulfilled life.

This, then, is the modern Indian woman: in a white cotton sari at one moment, carrying out an age-old ritual with an attention to detail that both absorbs and animates her, and in a pair of blue jeans at another time, sprawled on a sofa in front of the television watching a soap on family intrigues with an intense interest that lights up her entire face. Hers is the driving force in the changes taking place in the Indian family, an institution that is inherently conservative and changes at a much slower pace than the political, economic and other institutions of society. Slowly but surely the middle-class woman is pushing the family towards a greater acknowledgement, grudging or otherwise, of the importance (if not yet the primacy) of the marital bond. A greater individuation of the child will be an inevitable consequence of this *psychological* nuclearization within the joint family, as also a boost in the pleasures and sorrows of individuality.

However, the coming centrality of the couple in Indian family life, already visible in the upper middle class, is also bound to be a source of strain on the modern marriage. As the psychoanalyst Otto Kernberg has pointed out, the paradox of the couple is that its intimacy is necessarily in opposition to the larger group and yet it needs this group for its survival.[25] It is only in opposition to the conventional morality of the family, its ideological ritualization of commitment to the joint family and family tradition, that a couple establishes its identity and begins its journey as a couple. A couple's intimacy is implicitly rebellious and defiant, it not only attracts sanctions from those who see themselves as representatives of the family order but also arouses guilt in the couple's constituents—the husband and/or the wife. The option of erasing the boundary with the family, re-embracing its ideological underpinnings and dissolving into the larger group to end the disquiet caused by the sanctions and the guilt, thus always remains tempting in the life of the couple. This is especially so with a couple which has already allowed a breaching of this boundary because of its children, since many Indian couples proceed on the unconscious assumption that parental functions should replace sexual ones once a child is born.

Some upper-middle-class couples seek a solution by cutting themselves off completely from the joint family. Here the danger is that the inevitable upsurges of aggression in the couple's relationship will have no other outlet and can cause serious damage to the marriage. The larger family mitigates the effects of aggression either by some of its members serving as the objects of its discharge or by providing the stage where the husband and wife can be aggressive towards each other in the relative safety of an intimate audience.

Moreover, living in close quarters with other couples in a

large family, with at least a pre-conscious awareness of their sexual lives (and observing its signs on the faces and bodies), is a constant source of excitement that can help in maintaining the couple's erotic life. The extended Indian family is not only a system of duties and obligations but also a highly charged field of eroticism. The danger, of course, is that one or the other family member—a sister-in-law, a brother-in-law, a cousin, a niece, a nephew—may come to constitute a sexual temptation that cannot be resisted by the man or the woman, thus destroying the couple's intimacy. But then, such danger is even greater in the social network of friends and colleagues that has begun to replace the family in the life of many middle-class couples. Especially since the tolerance for such lapses is generally less than if they had taken place within the family.

These are the inevitable pressures and challenges of our changing world. Only the future will tell whether the Indian woman's long cherished wish to constitute a 'two-person universe' with her husband will not degenerate (as it has done in some Western marriages that have become fortresses which shut out all other relationships) into a mutual ego boosting, a joint self-centeredness, a *folie à deux* of a special kind.

# SEXUALITY

*There* are very few aspects of Indic civilization where the disjunction between its 'classical' and 'modern' ages is as striking as in the area of sexuality. Compared to the conservative sexual attitudes and oppressive mores of today, the stance of ancient Hindus towards the erotic and sensual life, at least as it comes to us in literary and scholarly texts, as also in temple sculptures, seems to belong to another galaxy. The terrain of ancient Indian sexuality is home to a siren's song to which most contemporary Indians continue to shut their ears.

## SEX IN ANCIENT INDIA

No discussion of Indian sexuality, ancient or modern, can begin without a respectful nod, or rather a bow, towards the *Kamasutra* which has been pivotal in forming the rest of the world's ideas on Indian sexuality. People who find it difficult to name one Sanskrit book, or are not even aware of the existence of Sanskrit as the classical language of ancient India, have no trouble in identifying the *Kamasutra*. The name alone conjures up 'titillating visions of erotic frescos in which regal maharajas with outsized genitals cavort with naked bejewelled nymphs in positions exotic enough to slip the discs of a yoga master.'[1]

Few, of course, have read this third-century treatise on erotic love, even the 'good' parts about positions in sexual intercourse that have given it the reputation of 'that racy sex manual from India'. What the *Kamasutra* is *really* about is the art of living—about finding a partner, maintaining power in marriage, committing adultery, living as or with a courtesan, using drugs—and also about positions in sexual intercourse. It has attained its classical status as the world's first comprehensive guide to erotic love because it is at bottom about essential, unchangeable human attributes—lust, love, shyness, rejection, seduction, manipulation—that are part of our sexuality.

The *Kamasutra* can be viewed as an account of a 'psychological war' of independence that took place in India some two thousand years ago. The first aim of this struggle, the rescue of erotic pleasure from the crude purposefulness of sexual desire, from its biological function of reproduction alone, has been shared by many societies at different periods of history. Today, the social forces and the moral orders that would keep sexuality tied to reproduction and fertility are no longer of such fateful import, at least not in what is known as the 'modern West' (and its enclaves in the more traditional societies around the world), although this was not the case even a hundred years ago.

The first European translators of the *Kamasutra* in the late nineteenth century, clearly on the side of sexual pleasure in a society where the reigning Christian morality sought to subordinate if not altogether eradicate it, regarded the ancient Sanskrit text, devoted to the god of love without even a nod to the divinities who preside over fertility and birth, as a welcome ally. To them, the *Kamasutra* was the product of a place and people who had raised the search for sexual pleasure to the status of a religious quest. Lamairesse, the French translator, even called it the '*Théologie Hindoue*' that revealed vital truths regarding man's fundamental, sexual nature, while

Richard Schmidt, the German translator, would wax lyrical: 'The burning heat of the Indian sun, the fabulous luxuriance of the vegetation, the enchanted poetry of moonlit nights permeated by the perfume of lotus flowers and, not in the least, the distinctive role the Indian people have always played, the role of unworldly dreamers, philosophers, impractical *Schwärmer*—all combine to make the Indian a real virtuoso in love.'[2]

Vatsyayana and other ancient Indian sexologists can certainly be viewed as flag bearers for sexual pleasure in an era where the sombre Buddhist view of life which equated the god of love with *mara* ('death', 'destruction') was still influential. But they were also inheritors of another world view, that of the epics, the *Mahabharata* and the *Ramayana*, where sexual love is usually a straightforward matter of desire and its gratification. This was especially so for the man, for whom a woman was an instrument of pleasure and an object of the senses—one physical need among many others. There is an idealization of marriage in the epics, yes, but chiefly as a social and religious act. The obligation of conjugal love and the virtue of chastity within marriage were primarily demanded of the wife, while few limits were set on a husband who lived under and looked up at a licentious heaven teeming with lusty gods and *apsara*s, the heavenly seductresses, otherworldly and utterly desirable at once, eager to give and take pleasure. The Hindu pantheon of the epics was not unlike the Greek Olympus where gods and goddesses sport and politic with a welcome absence of moralistic subterfuge.

Vatsyayana and the early sexologists were thus also heirs to a patrimony where sexual desire ran rampant, unchecked by moral constraints. Indeed, Shvetaketu Auddalaki, the legendary composer of the first textbook on sex, was credited with trying to put an end to unbridled sexual coupling and profligacy in relation to intercourse with married women which is so prominent in the *Mahabharata*. Prior to Shvetaketu's treatise, both married and unmarried women were viewed as items for indiscriminate consumption, 'like cooked rice'. Shvetaketu was the first to make the novel suggestion that men should not generally sleep with the wives of others.

Besides the rescue of erotic pleasure from the confining morality of fertility and reproduction, the *Kamasutra*'s 'freedom struggle' thus also had a second aim. This was to find a haven for the erotic from the ferocity of unchecked sexual desire. For desire has an open, lustful intent, imperiously and precipitously seeking satisfaction for its own sake, a tidal rush of gut instinct. Human beings have always sensed that sexual desire may also have other aims besides the keen pleasure of genital intercourse and orgasm. For instance, sexual fantasies of men and women are often coloured with the darker purposes of destructive aggression. Without an imagined violence, however minimal, attenuated and distant from awareness, many men fail to be gripped by powerful sexual excitement. Aggressiveness towards the woman is as much a factor in their potency as their loving feelings. One of their major fantasies is of taking by force that which is not easily given. Some imagine the woman not wishing to participate in the sexual experience but then being carried away by the man's forcefulness despite herself. We find a variant of the 'possession fantasy' in classical Sanskrit love poetry, with its predilection for love scenes where the woman trembles in a state of diffuse bodily excitement as if timorously anticipating a sadistic attack, her terror a source of excitement for both herself and her would-be assailant. In Kalidasa's *Kumara Sambhava*, a fourth-century masterpiece of erotic poetry, Shiva's excitement reaches a crescendo when Parvati 'in the beginning felt both fear and love'.[3]

Sexual desire, in which the body's wanting and violence, the excitement of orgasm and the exultation of possession, all flow together, then, can easily overwhelm erotic pleasure.

Today, when what were once called 'perversions' are normal fare of television channels, video films and Internet sites, where small but specialized professions exist for the satisfaction of every sexual excess, the *Kamasutra*'s second project of rescuing the erotic from the rawly sexual would find many supporters. In today's post-moral world, the danger to erotic pleasure is less from the icy frost of morality than from the fierce heat of instinctual desire. The *Kamasutra*'s most valuable insight is that pleasure needs to be cultivated, that in the realm of sex, nature requires culture.

Culture, in the *Kamasutra*'s sense the sixty-four arts that need to be learnt and so on, needs leisure and means, time and money. These were not in short supply for the text's intended audience, an urban (and urbane) elite consisting of princes and barons, high state officials, and wealthy merchants who had the leisure time to seduce virgins and other men's wives and a considerable amount of money to buy the gifts needed for the purpose.

Despite the role of violence in sexuality, the feeling-tone of the *Kamasutra*'s eroticism is primarily of lightness. In its pages, we meet leisured gallants who spend hours in personal grooming and teaching their mynah birds and parrots to speak. Their evenings are devoted to drinking, music and dance; that is, when they are not busy talking poetry and engaging in sexual banter with artful courtesans. In its light-hearted eroticism, the *Kamasutra* is part of a literary climate during the first six centuries of the Christian calendar where the erotic was associated with all that was bright, shining and beautiful in the ordinary world. The Sanskrit poems and dramas of this period are also characterized by this lightness, an eroticism more hedonist than impassioned. The mood is of a playful enjoyment of love's ambiguities, a delighted savouring of its pleasures, and a consummately refined suffering of its sorrows. The poems are cameos yielding glimpses into arresting erotic moments, their intensity enhanced by the accumulation of sensuous detail. The aesthetic of this period could confidently proclaim that certain emotions such as laziness, violence and disgust do not belong to a depiction of the erotic. Today the 'flavour' or 'essence'—*rasa*—of sexual love knows no such limits.

## Women in the *Kamasutra*

Another aspect of the *Kamasutra* is the discovery of the woman as a subject and full participant in sexual life. The text both reflects and fosters the woman's enjoyment of her sexuality. Vatsyayana expressly recommends the study of his book to women, even before they reach puberty. Two of the book's seven parts are addressed to women, the fourth to wives and the sixth to courtesans. The woman is very much a subject in the erotic realm, not a passive recipient of the man's lust. Of the four embraces in preliminary love-play, the woman takes the active part in two. In one she encircles her lover like a vine does a tree, offering and withdrawing her lips for a kiss, driving the man wild with excitement. In the other—familiar from its sculpted representation in the temple friezes of Khajuraho—she rests one of her feet on the man's and the other against his thigh. One arm is across his back and with the other clinging to his shoulder and neck she makes the motion of climbing him as if he were a tree. In the final analysis, though, given the fact that the text was composed by a man primarily for the education of other men, the fostering of a woman's sexual subjectivity is ultimately in the service of increasing the man's pleasure. The *Kamasutra* recognizes that a woman who actively enjoys sex will make it much more enjoyable for her male partner.

Women in the *Kamasutra* are thus not only presented as erotic subjects but as sexual beings with feelings and emotions which a man needs to understand for the full enjoyment of erotic pleasure. The third part of the text instructs the man on a young girl's need for gentleness in removing her virginal fears and inhibitions. Erotic pleasure demands that the man be pleasing to his partner. In recommending that the man not sexually approach the woman for the first three nights after marriage, using this time to understand her feelings, win her trust and arouse her love, Vatsyayana takes a momentous step in the history of Indian sexuality by introducing the notion of love in sex. He even goes so far as to advance the radical notion that the ultimate goal of marriage is to develop love between the couple and thus considers the love-marriage, ritually considered 'low' and disapproved of in the religious texts—and still a rarity in contemporary Indian society—as the pre-eminent form of marriage.

The *Kamasutra* is a radical advocate of women's empowerment in a conservative, patriarchal society in other ways too. The law books of the time come down hard on women contemplating divorce: 'A virtuous wife should constantly serve her husband like a god, even if he behaves badly, freely indulges his lust, and is devoid of any good qualities.'[4] Vatsyayana, on the other hand, views the prospect of wives leaving their husbands with equanimity; he tells us that a woman who does not experience the pleasures of love may hate her man and leave him for another. He is equally subversive of the prevailing moral order between the sexes when he advises courtesans (and, by extension, other women readers of the text) on how to get rid of a man she no longer wants:

> She does for him what he does not want, and she does repeatedly what he has criticized...She talks about things he does not know about...She shows no amazement, only contempt, for the things he does know about. She punctures his pride. She has affairs with men who are superior to him.

She ignores him. She criticizes men who have the same faults. And she stalls when they are alone together. She is upset by the things he does for her when they are making love. She does not offer him her mouth. She keeps him away from between her legs. She is disgusted by wounds made by nails or teeth when he tries to hug her, she repels him by making a 'needle' with her arms. Her limbs remain motionless. She crosses her thighs. She wants only to sleep. When she sees that he is exhausted, she urges him on. She laughs at him when he cannot do it, and she shows no pleasure when he can. When she notices that he is aroused, even in the daytime, she goes out to be with a crowd.

She intentionally distorts the meaning of what he says. She laughs when he has not made a joke, and when he has made a joke, she laughs about something else...'[5]

Yes! That would get rid of him!

It is not that Vatsyayana idealizes women; only that he is equally cynical about men and women as far as sex is concerned. The Hindu law books are traditionally patriarchal in discussing why women commit adultery: 'Good looks do not matter to women, nor do they care about youth; "A man!" they say, and enjoy sex with him, whether he is good-looking or ugly.'[6] The *Kamasutra*, on the other hand, is more egalitarian: 'A woman desires any attractive man she sees, and, in the same way, a man desires a woman. But, after some consideration, the matter goes no further.'[7]

## Love in the age of the *Kamasutra*

The erotic love of the *Kamasutra* is not of the romantic variety as we know it today. Its tenderness and affection for the partner is still, largely, in the service of sexual desire. Thus Vatsyayana's detailed instructions to the man on the tender gestures required of him at the end of sex, 'when their passion has ebbed', end with the words, 'Through these and other feelings, the young couple's passion grows again.'[8] The literary birth of romantic love—in the twelfth century: Bedier's *The Romance of Tristan and Iseult* in Europe and Nizami's *The Story of Layla and Majnun* in the Islamic world—still lay far in the future.

What distinguishes romantic love from the erotic love of the *Kamasutra* is the pervasive presence in the former of what may be called 'longing'. In its quest for oneness with the beloved, longing emphasizes a willing surrender to and adoration and cherishing of the person for whom one lusts. Longing presupposes, first, a special kind of identification that makes the person of the beloved attain for the lover a centrality at least equal to his own. It also requires an idealization which makes him experience the loved one as an infinitely superior being to whom he willingly subordinates his desire. Romantic love finds fulfilment only when the lover becomes metaphorically porous to the beloved. Possessive desire aspires to overpower its object while tender longing would have her or him indestructible; longing lends desire permanence and stability.

The porosity, the surrender, the identification and the idealization, are not a part of the erotic love we find in the *Kamasutra* or, for that matter, in the classical literature of that period. In Sanskrit and Tamil love poems, as in the textbooks of erotics, the beloved is a partner who is a source of excitement and delight, enlivening the senses but not a beacon for the soul. She is to be explored thoroughly, in enormous detail, and therefore she is not quickly abandoned. Yet her inner life or her past and future are not subjects of entrancement; the impulse is not of fierce monogamy.

For most modern readers who have an affinity for the personal and the subjective, this emphasis on love as a depersonalized voluptuous state, while delighting the senses, does not touch the heart. For those whose sensibility has been moulded by romanticism and individualism it is difficult to identify with the impersonal protagonists of the poems. These are not a *particular* man or woman but man and woman as such—provided he is handsome, she beautiful, and both young. The face of the heroine, for instance, is always like a moon or lotus flower, eyes like water lilies or those of a fawn. She always stoops slightly from the weight of her full breasts, improbable fleshy flowers of rounded perfection that do not even admit a blade of grass between them. The waist is slim, with three folds, the thighs round and plump, like the trunk of an elephant or a banyan tree. The navel is deep, the hips heavy. These lyrical yet conventional descriptions of body parts seem to operate like collective fetishes, culturally approved cues for the individual to allow himself to indulge erotic excitement without the risk of surrender so longed for in romantic love.

Whereas the erotic love of the *Kamasutra* and the classical Sanskrit literature of the period is bright and shiny, romantic love, in spite of its exquisite transports of feeling, is often experienced by the lovers as dark and heavy. In its full flowering, sexual desire loses its primacy as the lover strives to disappear in the contours of another, a person whose gender fits the mould but whose flesh is almost incidental to the quest for wholeness.[9] Sexual desire becomes a mere vehicle for a yearned for merger of souls, a consummation that is impossible as long as lovers have bodies. The impossibility of merger, making the lovers aware of their elemental separation, is the potential tragedy of romantic love, its anguish and torment. This is its inherent heaviness wherein lovers through the ages, and not only fictional ones, have cursed it as a plague and an affliction.

The suffering of erotic love, on the other hand, the dark spot on its brightness, has less to do with the soul's elemental longing to end separation than with the bodily nature of sexual desire. Sexual desire does not subside with seeming satiation. Memory as well as deliciousness of pleasure's ache gnaw further, making for the distress that marks the separation of lovers in erotic love. This sentiment casts only a small shadow on the *Kamasutra*, where it takes the rather different form of the sufferings of the rejected wife and the anxiety of the not-yet-successful suitor. The erotic love of the *Kamasutra* is then a precarious balancing act between the possessiveness of sexual desire and the tenderness of romantic longing, between the disorder of instinctuality and the moral forces of order, between the imperatives of nature and the civilizing attempts of culture. It is a search for harmony in all the opposing forces that constitute human sexuality, a quest often destined to be futile by the very nature of the undertaking. As Vatsyayana remarks: 'When the wheel of sexual ecstasy is in full motion, there is no textbook at all, and no order.'[10]

## Sexuality in the temples and literature of medieval India

From all available evidence—and the *Kamasutra* provides the bulk of it—there was little sexual repression in ancient India, at least among the upper classes, the *Kamasutra*'s primary audience. The demands of sexuality had to be reconciled with those of religion, yes, but it was reconciliation rather than suppression when the two were in conflict. The uninhibited sexuality of the *Kamasutra* where nothing is taboo in imagination and very little in reality, which combines tenderness with playful aggressiveness in lovemaking, where gender roles in the sexual act are neither rigid nor fixed, is brought to its visual culmination in the temples of Khajuraho.

This group of originally over eighty temples, of which twenty-nine still stand, was rediscovered in a village in central India in the middle of the nineteenth century. The sculptures and friezes of the temples, built between the tenth and eleventh centuries, are generally regarded as being among the masterpieces of Indian art and architecture. Besides the religious motifs, the temple walls also represent the world of the worshippers and portray life in all its fullness. Temples of this time were not only places of worship. They were centres of social, cultural and political life where musical and dance performances were held, literary and religious discussions took place and people met to discuss community issues.

Khajuraho's contemporary fame, even notoriety, however, is chiefly due to its profusion of erotic carvings. Among the most beautiful are the *apsara*s in a variety of moods and in various states of undress, exposing themselves with erotic suggestiveness. Then there are graphic depictions of sexual intercourse, group orgies and sex with animals. If there is one clear and unambiguous message in the sensuality of the sculpted representations of Khajuraho and Konarak, it is that the human soul is pre-eminently amorous, and nothing if not amorous.

The loving couple (the so-called mithuna motif) occurs in Indian temples from very early times, at least from the third century BC. The couple may well represent the union of the individual soul with the Supreme Soul—the highest goal of Hindu religiosity. A necessary auspicious element in Indian temples, the loving couple becomes elaborated through the centuries. By the time of Khajuraho, the artistic imagination of the temple sculptors had begun to depict the couple as one engaged in sexual intercourse. The progress from the more abstractly loving couple to the one engaged in intercourse is possible because the sexual act in Hindu tradition does not lie outside but within the holiness of life. As an authoritative religious text asserts, 'The whole universe, from Brahman to the smallest worm, is based on the union of the male and female. Why then should we feel ashamed of it, when even Lord Brahma was forced to take four faces on account of his greed to have a look at a maiden?'[11]

We must remember that the Indian combination of religiosity and eroticism is not unique to Khajuraho. From the ninth to the thirteenth century, when there was a remarkable spurt in temple building activity all over India, erotic sculptures were common. The infusion of religion with sexuality is not limited to sculpture but also extends to literature, pre-eminently the poetry and songs of bhakti, the devotional religiosity that first emerged in the sixth century in the south and then went from strength to strength to become the dominant form of Hindu religious expression all over the country. Bhakti's principal mood has always been erotic, extolling possessing and being possessed by the god as its ideal state. Here, religion is not an enemy of erotic sentiment but its ally. Even the highest of gods delights in the many hues of sexuality as much as mortals do. In Jayadeva's *Gita Govinda*, perhaps the swansong of this era which was coming to an end by the twelfth century, after their ecstatic lovemaking has subsided in orgasmic release, a playful Radha (the emblem of the human soul) asks Krishna (an incarnation of the divine) to rearrange her clothes and tousled hair:

'Paint a leaf on my breasts,
lay a girdle on my hips,
twine my heavy braid with flowers,
fix rows of bangles on my hands
and jewelled anklets on my feet.'
Her yellow-robed lover
did what Radha said. [12]

Jayadeva, legend has it, hesitant to commit sacrilege by having god touch Radha's feet, a sign of abnegation, had been unable to write the last lines and had gone out to bathe; when he returned he found that Krishna himself had completed the verse in his absence...

Bhakti poetry's erotic love for Krishna (or Shiva in Tamil or Kannada poetry), similar to the sentiments expressed toward

Jesus by such female medieval mystics as Teresa of Avilla, is not an allegory for religious passion but *is* religious passion; the Indian poets refuse to make a distinction between the religious and the erotic.

The sculptures of Khajuraho, Konarak and other medieval Indian temples, as also the erotic transports of bhakti poetry, do not need fanciful explanations. They are the art of and for an energetic and erotic people. As we look back over the centuries, the Indians of a bygone era are involved in the metaphysical questions raised by death, certainly. Yet they do not let the search for answers dominate the living of their lives; nor do they withdraw from life's possible joys because of the probable sorrows. Khajuraho represents the attitude of a people who, as Vatsyayana remarked centuries earlier, have doubts about the rewards of austerities and an ascetic way of life and believe that 'better a dove today than a peacock tomorrow'.

### CONTEMPORARY SEXUALITY

Between the land of the *Kamasutra* and contemporary India lie many centuries during which Indian society managed to enter the dark ages of sexuality. Modern, urban Indians, feasting their eyes on the erotic gyrations of scantily clad women in Bollywood movies, and fed on a steady diet of stories and surveys in the English-language media that proclaim a sexually rising India, may find it hard to believe that vast stretches of contemporary India remain covered in sexual darkness. In spite of the somewhat more relaxed attitudes in the upper and upper-middle classes, Indian sexuality remains deeply conservative if not puritanical, lacking that erotic grace which frees sexual activity from the imperatives of biology, uniting the partners in sensual delight and metaphysical openness.

Many observers wonder as to what could have happened to the same people who produced the *Kamasutra* to turn contemporary Indian eroticism into a sexual wasteland, a country where till recently kissing was banned in films yet where temple panels in Khajuraho and Konarak blithely show the pleasures of oral sex. Some blame the Muslim invasions and the medieval Muslim rule, although there is little evidence that Islam is a sexually repressive creed. At least in the upper classes, sexual love in most Islamic societies has been marked by a cheerful sensuality.[13] Indeed, a number of hadiths, the commentaries on the Quran, strongly favour the satisfaction of the sexual instinct. At least, that is, for the privileged male.

Others blame the Victorian morality of British colonial rule, itself the consequence of Christianity's uneasy relationship with the body, for a state of affairs where modern Indians are embarrassed by Khajuraho's sculptures and feel the need to explain them away in convoluted religious metaphors and symbols or to dismiss them as products of a 'degenerate' era.

For the 'fault', if it can be called one, one must look within Hindu culture itself, to its holding fast to the ascetic ideal and the virtues of celibacy. At the same time that the *Kamasutra* came into existence, there were other texts painting scary pictures of what the loss of semen could entail for the man and elaborating a whole mythology of the woman 'draining' the man in the sexual act. This near-primal fear, intimately linked with the Hindu concept of purity and impurity, results from the belief that what is most pure needs the greatest protection. Semen, the purest bodily product of a man and the source of his power, needs to be protected from the woman's ferocious and insatiable desire. Innumerable myths equate bodily weakness or loss of spiritual power in a man or a god with the loss of semen. These myths and legends vividly demonstrate why the ideals of sexual restraint and celibacy enjoy such a high status in Indian culture. In the ascetic imagination, women and their power to attract men is a temptation that is feared the most. This is an imagination scarred by the threat posed by women who are regarded as lustful and sexually rapacious by nature; that is, as long as they have not become mothers.

The ascetic ideal, too, is then quintessentially Indian, perennially in competition with the erotic one for possession of the Indian soul. It is very unlikely that ancient Indians were ever, or even could be, as unswerving in their pursuit of pleasure as, for instance, the ancient Romans. Although today there are again signs of a change, a tentative re-emergence of the erotic among the upper-class urban elite, the strain of asceticism, the road to spirituality through celibacy, held aloft through centuries by the Hindu version of William Blake's 'priests in black gowns...binding with briars my joys and desires', has dominated Indian sexual discourse for the last few centuries.

## Sexuality and health

One of the ways the ascetic discourse has sought to assert its pre-eminence over the erotic one is by associating sexuality with fears relating to health. By this we do not only mean diseases that the Hindu medical tradition explicitly relates to sexuality—for instance, 'overheating' due to too much sex leading to venereal disease, or sexual intercourse with a menstruating woman and adultery causing a variety of physical and mental diseases.

The relation between sexuality and ill health in the ascetic discourse is more complex than a simple matter of the sexual origin of diseases. Indeed, the ascetic imagination often seems to be obsessed with sex, for instance in the frequent and long descriptions of the dramatic combat of celibate yogis with the god of desire—assisted by his host of beautiful apsaras—while they seek to conquer and transform their sexuality into spiritual power. In traditional ascetic discourse, spirituality is intended to be an intensely practical affair, concerned with the 'alchemy' of the libido that would transform it into spiritual power. It is the sexual fire that stokes the alchemical transformation, wherein the cooking pot is the body and the cooking oil is a distillation from sexual fluids.

In its popular form, the theory of sexual sublimation goes something like this: Physical strength and mental power have their source in *virya*, a word that stands for both sexual energy and semen. Either virya can move downward in sexual intercourse, where it is emitted in its gross physical form as semen, or it can move upward through the spinal chord and into the brain in its subtle form known as *ojas*. Semen, we should note here, is the meeting point of medicine and spirituality. Indeed, for Sushruta, the author of one of the two foundational texts of traditional Indian medicine, Ayurveda, semen is the material form of the individual soul.

Ascetic discourse regards the downward movement of sexual energy and its emission as semen as enervating, a waste of vitality and essential energy. Of all the emotions, it is said, lust throws the physical system into the greatest chaos, with every passionate embrace destroying millions of red blood cells. The physiology of Ayurveda maintains that food is converted into semen in a thirty-day period by successive transformations (and refinements) through blood, flesh, fat, bone and marrow till semen is distilled—forty drops of blood producing one drop of semen. Each ejaculation involves a loss of half an ounce of semen, which is equivalent to the vitality produced by the consumption of sixty pounds of nourishing food. In another calculation with similar pedagogic intent, each act of copulation is equivalent to an energy expenditure of twenty-two hours of concentrated mental activity or seventy-two hours of hard physical labour.

On the other hand, if semen is retained, converted into ojas, and moved upward by observing celibacy, it becomes a source of spiritual life rather than a cause of physical decay. Longevity, creativity, and physical and mental vitality are enhanced by the conservation of semen; memory, will power, inspiration—scientific and artistic—all derive from celibacy. The belief in the possibility of sublimating sexuality into spirituality is shared by most Hindus—Mahatma Gandhi was only one of its best-known advocates and practitioners.

Of course, given the horrific imagery of sexuality as cataclysmic depletion, no people can procreate with any sense of joyful abandon unless they develop a good deal of scepticism in relation to the sexual prescriptions and ideals of this discourse which for centuries has continued to constitute the cultural 'superego' of Hindus, shared by saints and sinners alike. The relief at seeing the fierce ascetic's pretensions humbled by the charms of a heavenly seductress—the apsara Menaka seducing the sage Vishwamitra, or Rambha causing Gautama to involuntarily ejaculate—belongs not only to the gods but is shared equally by the mortals who listen to the myth or see it enacted in popular dance and folk drama. The ideals of celibacy are then simultaneously subscribed to and scoffed at. There are a number of sages in the Hindu tradition (Mahatma Gandhi being the latest addition to that assemblage) who are admired for their successful celibacy and the power it brought them. There are, however, also innumerable folk tales detailing the misadventures of randy ascetics. In the more dignified myths, even the Creator is laid low by his carnal wishes.

The heavenly nymph Mohini fell in love with the Lord of Creation, Brahma. After gaining the assistance of the god of love, Kama, she went to Brahma and danced naked before him. Brahma remained unmoved till Kama struck him with one of his flower-arrows. Brahma's protests that he was an ascetic who must avoid all women, especially prostitutes, steadily grew weaker. Mohini laughed and insisted that he make love to her and pulled at his garment, revealing his aroused state. The sages who found them together questioned the Creator as to how Mohini had come to be in his presence. At first the Creator tried to conceal his shame by dissembling, 'She danced and sang for a long time and then when she was tired she came here like a young girl to her father.' But the sages laughed, for they knew the whole secret, and Brahma laughed too.[14]

The ultimate if ironic refinement of celibacy is found in the mystical practices of Tantra, where the aspirant is trained and enjoined to perform the sexual act without desire, controlling ejaculation at the very last moment, thus divorcing the sexual impulse from human physiology. The impulse, it is believed, stirs up the semen in this ritual and unbelievably passionless sexual act and gives birth to energies that can be channelled upward to bring spiritual benefit.

Our scepticism in relation to celibacy does not mean its unqualified rejection. We would agree with Thomas Mann that efforts to sustain a renunciation of sexual love are worthy of respect, for they deal with the spiritual and thus with the pre-eminently human. We would also, like Freud, concede the possibility of successful celibacy to a few extraordinary people of genuine originality and with a self-abnegating sense of mission or transcendent purpose. Our difficulty with celibacy is its elevation as a cultural ideal for a whole people, which then plays a vital role in the production of anxiety, associated with the 'squandering of the sperm', as it does in many Indian men. Indeed, there is a singular disease particular to South Asia called svapnadosha (literally, 'dream fault'). In this 'cultural sickness', young men complain of body aches and headaches, increasing enervation, and feelings of unreality about the body because of loss of semen in nocturnal emissions.

## Virgins and others

Sexuality is notorious for not conforming to the commands of the culture's moral guardians. Especially in the young, its unruliness has a tendency to seep through the crevices in the walls of culture. Although Indian mores taboo any expression of adolescent sexual behaviour before marriage, various studies from different parts of India suggest that the injunction is flouted by twenty to thirty per cent of the young men.[15] It is more successful in the case of young women, urban or rural, affluent or poor, where these studies report premarital sexual activity in less than ten per cent of the young women. The greater incidence of sexual activity reported by young men is due to the fact that their sexual partners not only include girls of their own age—both 'time pass' and 'true love' affairs, but also commercial sex workers and older married women in the neighbourhood whom they call 'aunties'.

A part of the gender difference in sexual behaviour during youth may also be the result of (boastful) over-reporting by men and (inhibited) under-reporting by women. Girls tend to be secretive about their sexual relationships since even the hint of a friendship with a boy can ruin their reputation, their marriage prospects and the social status of their families. If asceticism is a way of controlling male sexuality, then chastity before (and faithfulness in) marriage are the inflexible checks on female sexuality.

Leaving aside a small upper-class crust in the metropolitan centres, chastity remains the highest commandment for the young unmarried woman. Whether she belongs to a protective, upwardly mobile middle-class family or lives in the slum of a large city, an Indian girl learns early in life that she must move and behave with utmost modesty in public spaces. In contrast to boys, girls who make even the slightest public show of sexual interest are not only risking their reputation but are also setting themselves up as prey for sexual harrassment. Families, too, as we saw earlier, severely limit a girl's interaction with boys who are not part of the family so as not to jeopardize her 'value' in the marriage market. An eighteen-year-old college student from Delhi says, 'If someone finds out that a girl has boyfriends, then—oh god!—no one will marry her because she may have gone to bed with them. A woman should only have sex after marriage.'[16] 'There is no problem if my brother had a girlfriend,' says another college student, 'but in my case it would be a scandal. If I got married tomorrow, the neighbours would say, That girl is a slut. She had boyfriends before marriage. My brother has no such problems...If one of us has a boyfriend, she would keep it a secret. Otherwise she won't be allowed to go to the telephone at home, not allowed to go out...nothing.'[17]

Little wonder that a number of women in psychotherapy report their first sexual contact with a male member of the extended family—uncle, cousin, even an older brother and, in the case of middle- and upper-class women, also with male servants. The contacts rarely extend to penetrative sex but are nevertheless carriers of considerable guilt as the women struggle to repress memories of their own excitement and curiosity-driven participation in episodes of obvious sexual abuse.

In the identity formation of most young women in India, the conflict between individual needs and social norms leads to persistent feelings of guilt around premarital sexual contact. Young girls develop strongly ambivalent feelings around their sexual identity and its bodily expression. Besides guilt, the (hidden) interest in sexuality can also lead to overpowering feelings of shame. These are expressed, for instance, in a marked embarrassment to talk of sexual matters. After a certain age, most girls have never been naked in front of their parents, and they probably won't ever be with their husbands either; nor will they watch sexually explicit scenes on television together with other, especially male, family members.

There *are* changes taking place in urban India. Young girls are developing a greater acceptance of their bodies. They have begun to place importance on clothes that accentuate body contours and are eager to inform themselves on the care and ornamentation of the body through television programmes and women's magazines. Yet this increasing body consciousness stops with deeply internalized feelings of shame around the genitals—one's own and those of the male. Many girls and young women from higher castes do not even have a name for their genitals. At the most, genitals are referred to obliquely— for instance as 'the place of peeing', though even this euphemism carries a strong emotional charge. A twenty-three-year-old Sikh patient, educated in England, did not have any trouble mentioning her sexual parts as long as she could do so in English. If asked to translate the words into her mother tongue, the language nearer her early bodily experience, she would either 'forget' the appropriate words or freeze into a long silence.[18] Sexual ignorance, of course, thrives in the socially mandated pall of silence. A college-educated patient believed well into her late teens that menstrual blood, urine and babies all came through the urethra. Another woman, brought up in a village and presumably more familiar with the 'barnyard' facts of life, realized with consternation only when giving birth to her first child that babies were not born through the anus as she had believed.

It is undeniable that in urban India, young girls move more freely in public spaces than was the case with the generation of their mothers. But it is also indisputable that public space remains a domain of men and there are few signs that this will change in the near future. The writer V. Geetha eloquently describes what other women can only confirm from their experience:

> For many of us, nothing captures men's relationship to space as much as the image of the man urinating unconcernedly on a busy thoroughfare, next to a girl's school building, at a street corner where buses turn, in a public park. Consider flashers: what is it that makes them flash their organs at

women, at girls? What notions of intimacy drive men to
whisper obscenities into the ears of girls and women on a
crowded bus and train? Or pinch their breasts and behinds?
Why do men's hands stray, almost unconsciously, as it were,
to their crotches, even if they are at a public meeting and on
stage? (Women, on the contrary would pull their saris tighter
over their breasts.) It is as if the public space they claim so
effortlessly as their own was defined by their penis and its
vagaries.'[19]

## Sexuality in marriage

With so many traditional women carrying the baggage of
shame and guilt in relation to their (sexual) bodies, with all the
images of insatiable women and the notions of sex being an act
that drains a man of power and vigour running riot in the male
cultural imagination, the omens for a joyful sexual life in the
average Indian marriage are not promising. It is difficult for a
man to abandon himself fully to erotic transports if his wife's
potential infidelity is a major theme in the popular proverbs of
his culture.[20] 'Only when fire will cool, the moon burn or the
ocean fill with sweet water will a woman be pure,' is one of
the many pronouncements on the subject. 'A woman is a
woman if she remains within bounds; she becomes a donkey
out of them,' say the Tamils. The proverbs in *praise* of wives
invariably and predictably address their maternal aspect as for
instance in this one, popular in Assam and Bengal—'Who can
belittle women? Women who bear children!' A Punjabi proverb
puts the husband's quandary and its solution in a nutshell: 'A
woman who shows more love for you than your mother is a
slut.'

Studies show that many Indian men have internalized such
proverbs to a considerable extent. Sentiments such as 'She
shouldn't talk to men other than me; and even to my brothers
and relatives only in my presence'[21] are commonly shared,

leading to widespread sexual jealousy that can on occasion verge on paranoia. Many women cannot even talk to their husbands about taking precautions against unwanted pregnancy without being accused of contemplating adultery.[22] It may well be that some men need this jealousy to stoke their possessive desire and thus heighten their pleasure in sex. The violent promptings of jealousy, though, tend to undermine eroticism, reducing sex to a need of the body alone and remove all controls on the husband's abusive behaviour.

Weighed down with a cultural burden of fear, shame and guilt, physical love in many traditional Indian marriages often tends to be a sharp stabbing of lust without the full force of energizing erotic passion. Interviews with low-caste poor women in Delhi reveal a sexuality pervaded by hostility and indifference rather than affection and tenderness.[23] Almost all women portrayed sexual intercourse as a furtive act in a cramped and crowded room, lasting barely a few minutes and with a marked absence of physical or emotional caressing. Most women found it painful or distasteful or both. It was a situation to be submitted to, often for fear of a beating. None of the women removed their clothes for the act since it is considered shameful to do so. Though some of the less embittered women still yearned for physical tenderness from the husband, the act itself was seen as a prerogative and a legitimate need of the male—'*Aadmi bolna chahta hai* (Man wants to speak).' Another metaphor for what in English is called 'lovemaking' is '*Hafte mein ek baar lagwa lete hain* (I get it done to myself once a week).' In its original Hindustani, the phrase has echoes of a weekly injection, painful, perhaps, but necessary for health. The most common expressions for intercourse are *kaam* and *dhandha*, work and business. Sexual intercourse for these women (and men) seems to be structured in terms of contractual and impersonal exchange relations, with the ever-present possibility of one party exploiting or cheating the other.

Studies from other parts of India confirm these observations. For young women of the poorer sections of society—still the vast majority of Indian women—the expectations from their sexual life and of a potential husband are minimal: '...he should not drink or beat me, and support me and the family.'[24] Most women report that they were unprepared for, and ignorant about, sexual intercourse until the first night with their husbands. Many experienced some form of sexual coercion and described their first sexual experience as traumatic, distasteful and painful, involving the use of physical force: 'It was a terrifying experience; when I tried to resist, he pinned my arms above my head. It must have been so painful and suffocating that I fainted.'[24] This India is indeed far removed from the country where, once, the *Kamasutra* guided the newly married man thus:

> For the first three nights after they have been joined together, the couple sleep on the ground, remain sexually continent, and eat food that has no salt or spices. Then, for seven days they bathe ceremoniously to the sound of musical instruments, dress well, dine together, attend performances, and pay their respects to their relatives. All of this applies to all the classes. During this ten-night period, he begins to entice her with gentle courtesies when they are alone together at night.
>
> The followers of Babhravya say, 'If the girl sees that the man has not made conversation [that is, sex] for three nights, like a pillar, she will be discouraged and will despise him, as if he were someone of the third nature [that is, a homosexual].' Vatsyayana says: He begins to entice her and win her trust, but he still remains sexually continent. When he entices her he does not force her in any way, for women are like flowers, and need to be enticed very tenderly. If they are taken by force by men who have not yet won their trust they become women who hate sex.[25]

In contrast to much popular Western fiction for women, the Indian 'romantic' yearning is not for an exploring of the depths of erotic passion, or for being swept off the feet by a masterful man. It is a much quieter affair and, when unsatisfied, this longing shrivels the emotional life of many women, making some go through life as mere maternal automatons. Others, though, react with an inner desperation where, as one woman put it, 'even the smell of the husband is a daily torture that must be borne in a silent scream.' The desired intimacy, forever subduing an antagonism between husband and wife, inherent in the division of sexes, is the real *sasural*—the husband's home—to which a girl looks forward after marriage and which a married woman keeps on visiting and revisiting in the hidden vaults of her imagination.

## A shadow on male sexuality

A recurrent theme in the psyche of many Indian men and one which has sexual consequences of varying degrees has to do with a very close mother–son relationship.[26] An Indian man tends to experience his mother almost totally as a 'good mother'. The proportion of Indian men who express or experience an active dislike or contempt for or fear of their mothers at a *conscious* level is infinitesimally small. This is strikingly apparent in psychotherapy where, in the beginning, patient after patient invariably portrays his mother as highly supportive and extremely loving. Virtually every popular depiction of mothers and sons—in art, popular fiction in various Indian languages, the autobiographies of famous Indian men, mainstream cinema, folk tales and legends and proverbs— corroborates the mother's sentimental prevalence. (It needs to be noted here that this idealized image of the 'good mother' is largely a male construction. Indian women do not sentimentalize their mothers in this way. For daughters, the mother is not an adored and adoring figure on a pedestal; she is a more earthy presence, not always benign but always *there*.) It may well be that the omnipresence of the mother in the male psyche is more open in India than in the West. As the late folklorist and poet A.K. Ramanujan has observed, Indian men tend to repress their independence from their mothers while, in contrast, Western men tend to repress their dependence.[27]

With the mother–son constellation described above, it is clear that a psychological separation from the mother becomes an especially difficult task for most Indian men. Forty-five years ago, in a study of the men of the Agarwal community in North India, only one-fifth of the men described themselves as being closer to their wives than to their mothers.[28] Today, the proportion of men saying that they feel closer to their wives, especially in urban middle-class India, would be higher, also because of the shame in admitting to what would now be regarded as a retrograde and hopelessly un-modern attitude. Today, the conflict between the mother-in-law and the generally more independent daughter-in-law is more difficult than in olden times when the loyalty of the son towards the mother was taken for granted. Unable to make the choice between wife and mother, many men often react by becoming emotionally detached from both.

The psychological 'clinch' between mother and son that is prolonged well into late childhood can result in an unconscious demand from the mother that the child serve as an object of her own unfulfilled desires and wishes, however antithetical they may be to his own. Faced with these intimations, the son may feel confused, helpless and inadequate, frightened by his mother's overwhelming nearness and yet unable, and unwilling, to get away. Some of these intimations are sexual, and given the contentious—and to many, offensive—nature of this statement, let us explain.

The fate of a traditional Indian girl's sexuality is a socially enforced progressive renunciation of her erotic needs. The birth of a child does not change this prescription; in fact, maternity often demands an even greater repudiation of a woman's erotic impulses. The familial and social expectation that she now devote herself exclusively to the child's welfare, the long period of post-partum taboo on sexual intercourse in many communities, a husband who is often emotionally unavailable—these are only a few of the social factors which dispose a young mother to divert the stream of her eroticism towards the infant son.

A mother's inner discontents are normally conveyed to her infant, wordlessly, in the daily intimacy of her contact with him. In Indian families, the mother's (and other women's) erotic feelings towards a male child are often openly expressed. The sight of a mother and other maternal figures in the family playfully fondling an infant son's genitals, even kissing the penis, to the accompaniment of much hilarity at the infant's pleasurable squirming, is not uncommon. The displacement of a woman's sexual longings from her husband to her son poses one of the most difficult problems for the boy to handle. The relief of his mother's tension may become as important to the child as the satisfaction of his own needs. At a certain point, the unconscious erotic wishes that infuse a mother's caretaking can arouse an intensity of feeling in the little boy that are beyond his capacity to cope with. The son's predicament is extreme: although he unconditionally needs the physical tending and emotional sustenance that at first only his mother or other maternal persons provide, he is wary of the intensity of her feelings for him (and of his for her) and unconsciously afraid of being overwhelmed by them. As the infant boy grows, he senses that he cannot do without his mother nor remove himself from her presence, but at the same time he is incapable of giving her what she needs. Although these conflicts, arising out of the complex mother–son relationship are present in all cultures, the psyches of a number of Indian men are especially marked by what we call an unconscious 'maternal enthrallment':

the wish to get away from the mother, together with the dread of separation; a fear of the mother one longs for so much; an incestuous desire coexisting with the dread inspired by assertive female sexuality.

Thus, underlying the conscious idealization of the mother as a paragon of unconditional love, many Indian men have a latent conviction that the feminine principle is lustful and rampant with an insatiable sexuality. This dark imagery pervades the pronouncements on women in Hindu law books and in treatises on morality. It is encountered in legends and folk tales that are replete with figures of older women whose appetites debilitate a man's sexual vitality. The son's primitive dread of a maternal sexuality that drains, devours and sucks dry is expressed in such proverbs as, 'Fire is never satisfied with fuel, the ocean is never filled with rivers, death is never satisfied by living beings and women are never satisfied with men.'

The anxiety around female sexuality is also evident in the mildly phobic attitude toward sexually mature women in many parts of India. An anthropological observation in a Hyderabad village of the mid 1960s—'Young men have a special fascination for adolescent girls "whose youth is just beginning to blossom". Young men who succeed in fondling "the unripe, half-developed breasts" of a girl and in having intercourse with one "whose pubic hair is just beginning to grow" easily win the admiration of their age-group'—still holds true.[29] The practice among women in many communities of shaving their pubic hair is not only dictated by the hygienic imperatives of a hot country, as the women will claim, but also by the men's unease with mature female genitalia and preference for pudenda that appear virginal. The vicious circle that spirals inwards in the psyche of many Indian men is, then, evident: mature women are sexually threatening to these men, which contributes to their 'avoidance behaviour' in intimate relations, which in turn causes the women to extend a provocative sexual presence towards their sons, which eventually produces adult men who fear the sexuality of mature women.

Two popular myths about the sons of the goddess Parvati clearly illustrate how maternal enthrallment can threaten the sexual integrity of the son as a man.

In a myth relating to Shiva's elder son, the god Skanda, who killed a mighty demon, Skanda is rewarded by his mother Parvati with the permission to amuse himself as he pleases. Skanda makes love to the wives of the gods and the gods are helpless to stop him. They complain to Parvati who decides to take the form of whatever woman Skanda is about to seduce. Skanda is ashamed, thinks 'The universe is filled with my mother' and becomes passionless. According to another myth, seeing a mango floating down the river, Parvati said to her two sons, Skanda and Ganesha, that whoever rode around the universe first would get the mango. Skanda impulsively mounted his golden peacock and went around the universe. Ganesha thought, 'What could my mother have meant by this?' He then circled his mother, worshipping her, and said, 'I have gone around my universe.' He received the mango.

### ALTERNATE SEXUALITIES

Except for a few persons belonging to the English-speaking elite in India's metropolitan centres, and most of them in the higher echelons of advertising, fashion, design, and the fine arts and the performing arts, men (and women) with same-sex partners neither identify themselves as homosexuals nor admit their sexual preference, often even to themselves. In other words, there are large numbers of men—some married—who have had or continue to have sex with other men, but only a minuscule minority are willing to recognize themselves as 'homosexual'.

The statement that there are hardly any homosexuals in

India and yet there is considerable same-sex involvement seems contradictory but simple to reconcile. Sex between men, especially among friends or within the family during adolescence and youth, is not regarded as sex but *masti*, an exciting, erotic playfulness, with overtones of the *mast* elephant in heat. Outside male friendship, it is a way to satisfy an urgent bodily need or, for some, to make money. Sex, on the other hand, is the serious business of procreation within marriage. Almost all men who have sex with other men will get married even if many continue to have sex with men after marriage. Sexual relations with men are not a source of conflict as long as the person believes he is not a homosexual in the sense of having an exclusive preference for men and does not compromise his masculine identity by not marrying and refusing to produce children. As a recent study tells us, 'Even effeminate men who have a strong desire for receiving penetrative sex are likely to consider their role as husbands and fathers to be more important in their self-identification than their homosexual behaviour.'[30] Ashok Row Kavi, a well-known gay activist, relates that when he was young and being pressured to marry by his family, especially by the elder sister of his father, he finally burst out that he liked to fuck men. 'I don't care whether you fuck crocodiles or elephants,' the aunt snapped back. 'Why can't you *marry*?'[31]

The cultural ideology that strongly links sexual identity with the ability to marry and procreate does indeed lessen the conflict around homosexual behaviour. Yet for many it also serves the function of masking their sexual orientation. It also denies them the possibility of an essential aspect of self-knowledge. Those with a genuine homosexual orientation subconsciously feel compelled to maintain an emotional distance in their homosexual encounters and thus struggle against the search for love and intimacy which, besides the press of sexual desire, motivated these encounters in the first place.

The 'homosexual denial', as we would like to call it, is facilitated by Indian culture in many ways. A man's behaviour has to be really flagrant, such as that of the cross-dressing *hijra*s, the community of transvestites, to excite interest or warrant comment. For some, the mythology around semen can serve as a cultural defence in denying their homosexual orientation. Kavi tells us about the *dhurrati panthi*s, men who love to be penetrated by other men because the semen inside them makes them twice as manly and capable of *really* satisfying their wives. Then there are the *komat panthi*s who like to give blow jobs but will not let themselves be touched. Some of these men are revered teachers, 'gurus', in bodybuilding gymnasiums (*akhara*s) who think they will become exceptionally powerful by performing oral sex on younger men. Both would be horrified if one called them homosexual.

Much of the contemporary attitude towards homosexuality goes back in time to ancient India where it was the homosexual but not homosexual activity that evoked society's scorn. In fact, in classical India the disparagement for the homosexual was not devoid of compassion. The homosexual belonged to a deficient class of men called *kliba* in Sanskrit, deficient because he is unable to produce male offspring. 'Kliba' was a catch-all term to include someone who was sterile, impotent, castrated, a transvestite, a man who had oral sex with other men, who had anal sex as a recipient, a man with mutilated or deficient sexual organs, a man who produced only female children, or, finally, a hermaphrodite. 'Kliba' is not a term that exists any longer but some of its remnants—the perception of a deficiency, and the combination of pity, dismay and revulsion towards a man who is unable to marry and produce children—continues to cling to the Indian homosexual.

In *Same-Sex Love in India*, Ruth Vanita argues that the relative tolerance, the grey area between simple acceptance and outright rejection of homosexual attraction, can be primarily attributed to the Hindu concept of rebirth.[32] Instead of condemning the couple, others can explain their mutual attraction as involuntary because it is caused by attachment in a previous birth. This attachment is presumed to have the character of an 'unfinished business' which needed to be brought to a resolution in the present birth. In ancient texts and folk tales and in daily conversations, mismatched lovers, generally those with vast differences in status (a fisherman or an 'untouchable' falling in love with a princess), are reluctantly absolved of blame and the union gradually accommodated because it is viewed as destined from a former birth. When a brave homosexual couple defies all convention by openly living together, its tolerance by the two families and their immediate society generally takes place in the framework of the rebirth theory. In 1987, when two policewomen in the state of Madhya Pradesh in central India got 'married', a *cause célèbre* in the Indian media, the explanation often heard from those who could no longer regard them as 'just good friends sharing living accommodation' was that one of them must have been a man in a previous birth and the couple were prematurely separated by a cruel fate.

In ancient India, homosexual activity itself was ignored or stigmatized as inferior but never actively persecuted. In the dharma (Moral Law) textbooks, male homoerotic activity is punished, albeit mildly: a ritual bath or the payment of a small fine was often sufficient atonement. This did not change materially in spite of the advent of Islam which unequivocally condemns homosexuality as a serious crime. Muslim theologians in India held that the Prophet advocated severest punishment for sodomy.[33] Islamic culture in India, though, also had a Persian cast wherein homoeroticism is celebrated in literature. In Sufi mystical poetry, in Persian and later in Urdu, the relationship between the divine and the human was expressed in homoerotic metaphors. Inevitably, the mystical was also enacted at the human level. At least among the upper classes of Muslims, the 'men of refinement', pederasty became an accepted outlet for a man's erotic promptings, as long as he continued to fulfil his duties as a married man.[34]

It seems that the contemporary perception of homosexual activity primarily in images of sodomy can be traced back to the Muslim period of Indian history. In ancient India, in the *Kamasutra* for instance, it is fellatio that is regarded as the defining male homosexual act. The fellatio technique of the closeted man of 'third nature' (the counterpart of the kliba in other Sanskrit texts) is discussed in considerable sensual detail whereas sodomy is mentioned in only one passage and that, too, in the context of heterosexual and *not* homosexual sex. It is the sodomy aspect of male homosexuality which the British colonial authorities, encased in a virulent, homophobic Victorian morality, latched on to in their draconian legislation of 1861. This law, Section 377 of the Indian Penal Code, states: 'Whoever voluntarily has carnal intercourse against the order of nature with any man, woman or animal shall be punished with imprisonment for life, or with imprisonment of either description for a term which may extend to ten years, and shall be liable to a fine.' The law, challenged in the courts by a gay organization and currently awaiting judgement in the Delhi high court, is still on the statute books. Although the law is rarely used to bring transgressors to court, it is regularly availed of by corrupt policemen to harass and blackmail homosexuals in public places.

If male homosexuals make themselves invisible, then lesbians simply do not exist in Indian society—or so it seems. Again, it is not as if Indians are unaware of lesbian activity. Yet this activity is never seen as a matter of personal choice, a possibility that is theoretically, if reluctantly, granted to 'deficient' men, the men of 'third nature', in ancient India. Lesbian activity is invariably seen as an outcome of the lack of sexual satisfaction in unmarried women, widows or women stuck in unhappy, sexless marriages. This is true even in the depiction of lesbian activity in fiction or movies. In Deepa Mehta's 1998 movie *Fire*, which caused a huge controversy, with Hindu activists setting fire to cinema halls because the movie showed two women having an affair, both women turn to each other only because they are deeply unhappy in their marriages.

In ancient India, lesbian activity is described in the *Kamasutra* at the beginning of the chapter on harems where many women live together in the absence of men. What the queens have is just one king, preoccupied with affairs of state, to go around. Since none of the kings can be the god Krishna who is reputed to have satisfied each one of his sixteen thousand wives every night, the women use dildos, as well as vegetables or fruits that have the form of the male organ. The implication is that lesbian activity takes place only in the absence of the 'real thing'. There are hints on other kinds of lesbian activity in the ancient law books: a woman who corrupts a virgin is to be punished by having two of her fingers cut off—a pointer to what the male author thinks two women do in bed. The harsh punishment is not for the activity itself but for the 'deflowering', the heinous crime of robbing a young girl of her chastity. It seems (and this is not surprising) that female homosexuality was punished more severely than homosexuality among men—out of concern for women's virginity and sexual purity, the traditionalists would say; to exercise control over women's sexual choice and activity, modern feminists would counter.

From medieval India we have the word *chapati* (sticking or clinging together) in Urdu, which is still used today to describe lesbian activity. A modern Hindi commentator on the *Kamasutra* captures the traditional liberal view (all traditionalists are not conservative!) of lesbianism in India when he writes: 'These days, the act of women rubbing their vulvas together is called *chapati*. Vatsyayana has discussed all natural and unnatural means for the satisfaction of unslaked sexual desires. But it is surprising he does not talk of *chapati* intercourse among unsatisfied queens. Perhaps *chapati* intercourse had not yet appeared at Vatsyayana's time; otherwise, it could not have remained hidden from his penetrating gaze. Today, when the emphasis on virginity has increased, the playing of *chapati* and the employment of artificial means for sexual satisfaction among girls is also increasing.'[35]

These, then, are some Indian variations on the universal theme of sexuality, that (to borrow from Melville) 'endless flowing river in the cave of man'. For sexuality is a country bounded by biological instinct on one side and the imaginative impulse on the other. Erotic spontaneity does not run wild in this terrain but is tamed by an imagination, pre-eminently cultural in origin, introducing fascinating paradoxes in the soul while the body seeks orgasmic release.

# HEALTH AND HEALING;
# DYING AND DEATH

𝑅amnath was a fifty-one-year old man who owned a grocery shop in the oldest part of Delhi. When he came for psychotherapeutic help he was suffering from a number of complaints, though he desired therapy for only one of them— an unspecified 'fearfulness', which became especially acute in the presence of his father-in-law. The anxiety, less than three years old, was a relatively new development. His migraine headaches, on the other hand, went back to his adolescence. Ramnath attributed them to an excess of 'wind' in the stomach which, he said, periodically rose up and pressed against the veins in his head. This diagnosis had been arrived at in consultation with doctors of traditional Indian medicine, Ayurveda, and the condition was treated with Ayurvedic drugs and dietary restrictions, as well as with liberal doses of aspirin.[1]

Ramnath had always had a nervous stomach, though it was never quite as bad as in the early months of his marriage some thirty years earlier. Then, he had suffered from severe stomach cramps and an alarming weight loss. He was first taken to a hospital by his father, where he was X-rayed and put through a battery of tests. Finding nothing wrong with him, the doctors had prescribed a variety of vitamins and tonics that had not been of much help. Older family members and friends had then recommended a nearby *ojha*—'sorcerer' is too fierce a translation for this mild-mannered professional of ritual exorcism—who diagnosed Ramnath's condition as the result of magic practiced by an enemy. The enemy was further identified as Ramnath's newly acquired father-in-law. The rituals to counteract the enemy magic were expensive, as was the yellowish liquid emetic prescribed by the ojha which periodically emptied Ramnath's stomach in gasping heaves. In any event, he was fully cured within two months of the ojha's treatment, and this particular problem had not recurred.

For the gradually worsening arthritic condition of his right elbow and wrist, Ramnath had turned to homeopathy after the obligatory but futile consultations with the 'allopath', as the Western-style doctor is called in India in contradistinction to practitioners of other medical systems. Homeopathy, too, had failed, and Ramnath had then consulted the priest-healer of a local temple who was well known for his expertise in curing pains of the joints. The priest prescribed a round of pujas together with dietary restrictions, such as the avoidance of yogurt and especially butter. The remedies had not worked.

Ramnath's 'fearfulness' had been treated with drugs by various doctors—allopaths as well as homeopaths, the *vaid*s of Ayurveda as well as the *hakim*s of Islamic Unani medicine. He had consulted psychiatrists, ingested psychotropic drugs and submitted to electroconvulsive therapy. He had gone through the rituals of two ojhas and was thinking of consulting a highly recommended third one.

The only relief came through the weekly *satsang*, the gathering of the local chapter of the Brahmakumari (literally, 'Virgins of Brahma') sect which he had recently joined. The communal meditations and singing gave him a feeling of peace, and his nights were no longer as restless. Ramnath was puzzled by the persistence of his anxiety and by his other ailments. He had tried to be a good man, he said, both according to the dharma of his caste and the limits imposed by his own character and predispositions. He had worshipped the gods and attended the service in the local temple with regularity, even contributing a generous sum toward the consecration of the Krishna idol in the temple of his native village in Rajasthan. He did not have any bad habits, he asserted. Tea and cigarettes, yes, but since a couple of years ago he had abjured even these minor though pleasurable addictions. Yet the anxiety persisted, unremitting, unrelenting.

Here, we are neither concerned with a psychological understanding of Ramnath's symptoms nor with the tracing of their genesis in his life history. Our purpose is to understand Ramnath's ailments and his efforts toward the restoration of well-being, against the background of his predominantly Hindu cultural tradition. In other words, the aim is to essay a cultural analysis rather than a psychoanalysis of Ramnath's condition, which will help us understand the nature of health and illness in the Indian setting.

At first glance, Ramnath's cognitive space in matters of illness and well-being seems incredibly cluttered. Gods and spirits, community and family, food and drink, personal habits and character, all seem to be involved in the maintenance of health. Yet these and other factors such as biological infection, social pollution and cosmic displeasure, all of which Indians would also acknowledge as causes of ill health, only point to the recognition of a person's simultaneous existence in many different orders of being. To use Western categories, from the first birth cry to the last breath, an individual exists equally in a *soma*, a *psyche* and a *polis*; in other words, a person is simultaneously a body, the self and a social being. Ramnath's experience of his illness may appear alien to non-Indians only because of the fact that the body, the self and the polis do not possess fixed, immutable meanings across cultures. The concept of the body and the understanding of its processes are not quite the same in India as they are in the West. The self—the Hindu 'subtle body'—is not primarily a psychological category in India, though it does include something of the Western 'psyche'. Similarly, for most traditional Indians, the polis consists not only of living members of the family and community, but of ancestral spirits, other spirit helpers, and— for the Hindus—the familiar gods and goddesses who populate the Indian cosmos.

Subjectively, then, an Indian is inclined to believe that his or her illness can reflect a disturbance in any one of the orders of being, whereas the symptoms may be manifested in the other orders. If a treatment, say in the bodily order, fails, one is quite prepared to reassign the cause of illness to a different order and undergo its particular curing regimen—without losing regard for other methods of treatment.

The involvement of all orders of being in health and illness also means that an Indian is generally inclined to seek more than one cause for illness in especially intractable cases. An Indian tends to view these causes as complementary rather than exclusive and arranges them in a particular order by identifying an immediate cause as well as peripheral and remote ones. The causes are arranged in concentric circles, with the outer circle including all the inner ones. To continue with our example, Ramnath, in concordance with Ayurvedic theory, which provides the governing paradigm for the explanation of physiological processes in traditional, Hindu India, may identify his arthritic pain as the result of a disequilibrium—what Ayurveda would call an imbalance of *dosha*s. He would see it, say, as an excess of *vayu* or 'wind', which needs to be brought back in the right balance through diet, drugs and external applications. The disequilibrium may be felt to be compounded by personal conduct—bad thoughts, habits—which, in turn, demand changes at the level of the self.

The fact that the disease persists or is manifested with a stubborn intensity may be linked with his astrologically 'bad times', requiring palliative measures, such as a *puja*. The astrological 'fault' will probably be further traced back to the bad karma of a previous birth about which, finally, nothing can be done—except, perhaps, the cultivation of a stoic endurance with the help of meditative practices.

Like most Hindus, Ramnath's image of his body and bodily processes, in which he would locate the first circle of any illness, is still governed by the precepts of Ayurveda, of which he may or may not be fully aware. Ayurveda is more than a traditional system of medicine. Ayurveda comprises the Indian notions of the constituents of the person and the nature of the body's connection with the psyche, the polis, the natural environment and the cosmos. These ideas constitute a cultural prism through which men and women in India have traditionally viewed the person and his or her state of well-being. As the Sri Lankan anthropologist Gananath Obeyesekere has remarked, 'Without some awareness of the theory of Ayurveda medicine it is not possible for us to understand much of what goes on in the minds of men in the South Asian world.'[2]

## THE BODY IN HEALTH AND ILLNESS IN AYURVEDA

Ayurveda is not unique in its intimate connection with the culture and society from which it springs. Medical theories, opinions and practices in any society tell us as much about social beliefs as about the art and science of healing. For instance, expensive medical procedures after the disease has run its course, or keeping alive a person in a coma with no hope of recovery, tell us something about the high value placed on technology in addressing problems that do not have a solution, the importance of the individual vis-à-vis the community (especially if the procedures have been financially ruinous for the family), the mechanistic conceptualization of the body, and so forth. In contrast to Western medicine, which is now global, Ayurveda has been less a mirror of society's cultural belief system than one of its chief architects. Its contribution to the shaping of Indian consciousness derives from its monopoly of the theory and practice of healing for scores of centuries till the nineteenth century, when this monopoly was challenged by Western medicine.

Not that Ayurveda remained in a mythically pure state till the colonial period. There have always been local deviations from the canonical texts, reflecting the influence of folk medical practices and, from the thirteenth century onwards, the impact of Islamic Unani medicine. Western, allopathic medicine, however, could not be easily accommodated in the Ayurvedic paradigm. Its challenge gave rise to modern Ayurveda, professionalized and institutionalized on the model of Western medicine and concerned with providing 'scientific' evidence for the efficacy of its healing methods and medicines. In recent decades, there has been a commercialization and standardization of Ayurvedic therapy, especially in its drugs for an urban middle class, and a transnational Ayurveda has emerged, one that has adapted parts of the traditional system, mainly pleasurable herbal oil massages and dietary advice, for an international clientele.

These modern developments go against the essence of classical Ayurveda and are vigorously resisted by some of the more traditional doctors. For them the storehouse of true knowledge is located in a remote golden past and only the ancient texts can be regarded as true teachers of this art and science of healing. It is precisely Ayurveda's 'unchanging' character, with the weight and authority of the past behind it, which testifies to its 'truth' and gives Ayurveda its legitimacy in Indian eyes. For Ayurvedic doctors, changing Western theories of disease—from disease as a consequence of faulty distribution of bodily fluids to the theory of autointoxication, from the concept of focal infection to the bacterial and viral origins of diseases—are then a search for the truth that Ayurveda has already discovered. The application of the standard criteria of science (for example, experimentation, falsification, quantification, concepts of proof other than authority) are thus irrelevant to Ayurveda since it operates with a model of a person quite different from one that underlies Western medicine.

The cornerstone of the Ayurvedic system are the *panchabhuta*—earth, fire, wind, water and ether—the 'five root forms of matter', the basic constitutive elements of the universe. Under certain favourable conditions, these elements become organized in the form of living creatures. These living creatures constantly absorb the five elements contained in environmental matter (nutrition), which is transformed by the fires in the body into a fine portion and into refuse, the three main forms of the latter being faeces, urine and sweat. Successive transformations of the fine portion of food produce the seven physiological elements (*dhatu*s) of the essence (rasa) of food— blood, flesh, bone, fat, marrow, semen, as well as the substances constituting the sense organs, body joints, ligaments, etc.—and the three *doshas*—*kapha*, *pitta* and *vata*. Since the Ayurvedic theory of illness and its cure hinges on the three doshas— translated variously as 'humours' (akin to the four Greek humours), 'metabolic principles', 'mind/body types', 'energy types' and 'irreducible body principles'—we need to understand them better.

When food first begins to be digested, a foamy kapha appears. When the food is half digested and passes into the intestine, a liquid substance called pitta appears. When the remnants of food reach the large intestine and begin to dry up, vata appears. Here's a simplified idea of how these three doshas are conceived of in Ayurveda:

Kapha is the controller of growth. It supplies moisture to

all body parts and maintains the immune system. In mental rather than physiological terms (remember the basic identity of body and mind in Ayurveda), kapha is associated with love and compassion when in balance and with insecurity and envy when out of balance.

Pitta governs the metabolic system. Mentally, in balance, it promotes intelligence and general satisfaction with life. Out of balance, it leads to outbreaks of rage.

Vata regulates body functions associated with breathing, circulation of blood and beating of the heart. It promotes creativity when in balance and causes anxiety and insomnia when out of balance.

Each human being has all the three doshas, although one or the other may predominate, making a person a kapha, pitta or vata type. The division of human beings into 'doshic' types is a testimony to Ayurveda's belief that, ultimately, medicine has to be completely attuned to the individual's body–mind make up, and its various categorizations are merely attempts to come as close to the uniqueness of the sick person as humanly possible.

Dominance of a particular dosha, though, is not disequilibrium. The three doshas play a supporting role in the body as long as they are in proper proportion and hence in balance. However, if a dosha becomes agitated and assumes abnormal proportions due to predisposing causes (which can range from wrong diet to environmental factors such as the weather, from psychological factors such as stress arising from disturbed family relationships to immoral conduct) it acts on the dhatus, the seven physiological elements of the body, producing disease. It is the task of the vaid, the Ayurvedic doctor, to re-establish the disturbed dosha balance, primarily through diet and drugs but also through oil massages and prescriptions relating to proper conduct and behaviour.

## A VISIT TO THE AYURVEDIC DOCTOR

To get a picture of Ayurveda in action and how its healers operate, let us describe Ramnath's (fictional) visit to a vaid for consultations. Guruji is a traditional Ayurvedic doctor who has a clinic on the ground floor of his two-storey house in the Sita Ram bazaar of old Delhi. Dressed in a white kurta and loose khadi pyjamas, a white turban wrapped around his head, Guruji is a sixty-year-old man with humorous eyes that belie the strictness of his manner. It is apparent that he is a man accustomed to commanding respect and deference.

Ramnath climbs up the three steps to the clinic and walks to Guruji's seat in the corner of the room, its floor covered with a thin white cotton mattress. The doctor is sitting cross-legged on the mattress, his back reclining against a thick round cushion pushed up against the wall. As Guruji watches Ramnath's nervous bird-like movements and looks at his thin frame, he is already speculating on Ramnath's doshic type—a vata perhaps? After Ramnath has described his physical complaint of arthritis in the right elbow and wrist, Guruji begins to gently question him. Does the pain get worse in any particular season or location? Any family history of the same ailment? Does the pain increase or decrease after taking any particular food?

Once the detailed history has been taken, which has given the doctor preliminary information on the predisposing causes, early indications, the symptoms and full extent of the disease, it is now time for a physical examination which will not only determine Ramnath's doshic profile but also indicate which of the doshas has got out of proportion to the others and what is the stage of the disease. Guruji is a firm believer in traditional wisdom and is particularly diligent in going through all the required steps. He begins with an overall physical examination recording his impressions of Ramnath's build, hair, nails, the colour and texture of his skin, the colour and sensitivity of parts of his tongue, the colour and consistency of his stool and urine (Ramnath has thoughtfully brought the samples along). Close questioning of Ramnath's habits, sleep and dreams follows as Guruji notes the characteristics of his patient's speech. All this—the *tattva pariksha*—is in service of determining Ramnath's basic mental make-up, whether he is of a *sattvic* temperament—calm, quiet and intelligent—or whether he is an active *rajasic* type—sensual and prone to impatience—or whether he is *tamasic*—lazy, dull and mentally unsteady. Ramnath is also closely questioned on his food preferences. A sattvic type likes sweet and agreeable tasting food, a rajasic type is partial to spicy, sour and bitter foods, and stale or half-cooked food devoid of its natural juices is the preferred tamasic fare. Ramnath answers all the questions and tells Guruji about his recurring fearfulness and bouts of forgetfulness.

Since food is of signal importance in the Ayurvedic scheme of things, questions on digestion now follow, the information collated with the results of the stool examination. The predominance of pitta makes for a fast digestion, of kapha for a slow one, while in the vata mode digestion can be either fast or slow. Ramnath admits to indigestion and a decreased appetite.

Now comes the most important part of the physical examination, the *naadi pariksha*, which roughly translates as 'examining the pulse', though naadi stands for both a nerve and an artery. According to Guruji, a good doctor can see the image of every important organ of the body reflected in the beat, movement and temperature of the naadi, a skill which like dancing or music can only be acquired through personal instruction by a good teacher combined with systematic practice. Although there are twenty-four clear naadis worthy of examination, the most frequently examined are the radial artery in the right wrist followed by the naadis in the fingers and the thumb. Except in cases of emergency, the examination must be conducted in the morning—hence Guruji's morning consultancy hours. This is due to the belief that the beat of the naadi is in its pure state in the morning after the night's rest; in the afternoon because of heat and in the evening because of the day's accumulated tensions, the natural beat of the pulse is likely to be contaminated.

The disturbance of a dosha is the minimum information a doctor gets from examining the pulse. An increase in vata makes the pulse unsteady, like the 'slithering of a snake'; an increase in pitta is reflected in a 'froglike hopping'; while an increase in kapha makes the pulse slow and steady 'like the gait of a hen'. There are different combinations of beat and movement of the naadi—the pulse signatures for various diseases, affected organs and emotional states, which a competent Ayurvedic doctor is supposed to be able to read. Moreover, in case of long-standing illness, a really good doctor is believed capable of predicting the time of a patient's death within a specified number of days, even hours, from the state of the naadi.

At last, Guruji is ready to make his diagnosis and prescribe the required treatment according to Ayurveda's concise dictum, 'Purify, pacify and remove the cause'. His diagnosis for Ramnath's disease is chronic *ama vata*, which he quietly explains to his puzzled patient. Ama is a toxic by-product of indigestion which is carried by an increased vata to kapha-dominated areas of the body like the joints, stomach and brain. Due to the imbalance of doshas, the ama becomes sticky and begins to block vital channels that nourish the body. Guruji's line of treatment is to increase the digestive fire to stop the production of ama, expel the already formed ama, reduce the inflammation of the joints and rejuvenate the affected joints at the wrist and elbow.

He prescribes two herbal drugs for increasing digestion and two drugs combining herbs and mineral compounds for reducing the inflammation of and rejuvenating the joints. He stands up and disappears into a room at the back which serves as his pharmacy and reappears after a while with a fortnight's supply of the drugs, each dose of each medicine wrapped separately in a piece of old newspaper. He cannot understand how people can take recourse to Ayurvedic drugs manufactured by pharmaceutical companies and sold over the counter in drug stores. These have a fixed-dose combination of herbs, plants and minerals whereas the whole basis of Ayurveda is to prescribe a drug individually according to the patient and the conditions of his life.[3]

Guruji is especially careful about the drugs containing mineral compounds. For although these drugs are easily available over the counter—millions of Indians, especially the urban middle class, use Ayurvedic preparations—he believes they can be dangerous in the absence of any quality controls and information on the methods of their manufacture. It is a myth, believed by most Indians, that Ayurvedic drugs are completely safe and have no harmful side effects. 'If a drug is effective, it is also dangerous,' he says, and quotes from memory from the *Carakasamhita*, the founding text of Ayurveda: 'A potent poison also becomes the best drug on proper administration. On the contrary, even the best drug becomes a potent poison if used badly.'

To get symptomatic relief from the pain in the joints, Guruji recommends that Ramnath have bi-weekly massages with sesame or mustard oil. Besides a cryptic 'Reduce worry and anxiety' and the more concrete 'Avoid late nights and afternoon naps', 'Always use hot water to bathe and drink' and 'Be very careful to have regular bowel movements', Guruji's advice in the area of personal conduct ends with 'Do not control any natural urge', giving Ramnath permission to belch or fart in public.

Guruji's most detailed prescriptions, though, are in the

area of diet. 'Avoid curds, milk, jaggery and constipating foods,' he tells Ramnath, not needing to spell out the latter which he assumes every Indian is familiar with from childhood. 'Consume chana dal, ginger, bitter gourd and drumsticks,' he continues. The 'juice of carrots, beet root and cucumber mixed together is recommended. Fruits like oranges, grapes and papaya are to be preferred. Soak half a teaspoon of garlic pods overnight in buttermilk, grind them into a paste in the morning and take it with a half a teaspoon of warm water on an empty stomach every day. Your spices of choice in cooking should be coriander and cumin.' We should note that in Ayurveda's striving to be a person- rather than disease-centered medicine, the prohibition of forbidden foods is not couched in terms of 'This and this is bad for all persons' but a more relative 'This is bad for certain kinds of persons, especially in a certain season.'

After Ramnath has left, Guruji is in the mood to talk about himself and his profession. He belongs to a vanishing breed of purists, he says. Most Ayurvedic physicians have few qualms about displaying the insignia of Western medicine—stethoscopes and thermometers for instance—in their consulting rooms. It is not really their fault, he concedes; many patients, especially in the rural areas, will not come to you if you don't give them injections.[4] Similarly, Ayurvedic medicines cannot be given in their traditional form as bitter decoctions, crude powders or hand-rolled pills but must come in modern dosage forms such as coated tablets, blister-packed capsules and syrups even if they are five times as expensive as their traditional counterparts.[5] This is what the modern middle-class consumers want, in their movies as in their medicines, indeed in their idea of themselves— Indian souls packaged in a slick Western style.

Turning more philosophical, Guruji continues: 'Medicine exists to fight diseases, not death. When death comes, holding hand with disease, then the doctor should prepare the patient for its arrival.

'The enemies of health are man's natural tendencies—greed, lust, anger and so on. You can conquer some but one or the other of the enemy always survives and it is he who brings death into the house of your life. Man lessens his lifespan due to his own sins and invites untimely death.'[6]

In the olden days, many patients asked for and accepted the tidings of their approaching death. An old potter, for instance, had once asked him during a sickness whether his time had come, so that he could return an outstanding loan before he departed from this world. Whatever the reason, the people of this country have always known that to go before your time has come is as great a sin as to try and cling to life when death is knocking at your door. A good death is an end that needs to be prepared for.

All this is changing with the advent of Western medicine, Guruji reflects. A Western-style doctor sees every sickness as a challenge to be overcome. And, indeed, the progress made by the technology of Western medicine is astonishing, although Guruji feels that perhaps its drugs are somewhat strong for the metal of which we in this country are made. Although he disapproves of modern manufacturers of traditional medicine, he would agree with one of their marketing managers who said that Ayurvedic and Unani medicines give Indians 'what they really are—their history, their culture and their health'.[7]

In any event, India and Indians are changing and there are not too many patients left like the old man he had tried to persuade the other day to go to the Moolchand hospital. 'If I have any life left, you will save me,' the man said. 'If not, then you will tell me well in advance and I will remember the goddess and make my preparations. As much as it is humanly possible, you will reduce my suffering. What else can a doctor do?'

## FOOD AND THE INDIAN MIND

There are few other people as concerned with food as Indians, especially the Hindus—not only with its preparation, but with the effect it has on the human body and mind. Thus, food taboos abound. Most of these beliefs have their source in Ayurveda, even when the person acting on them is unaware of this origin. With the postulated equivalence of the body and the universe, the microcosm and the macrocosm, as far as their basic constitutive elements—the five bhutas of air, water, earth, fire and ether—are concerned, a person is literally what he eats. Diet is viewed as the mainstay of physical and mental health—as also the cause of disease. The basic principle is that diet should contribute to the balance of the human body, mimicking the universal balance around it. Such balance can only be achieved by consuming the right foods at the right time in the right season and avoiding incompatible foods, thus compensating for the dominance of or the disproportionate increase in a particular dosha.

Foods (and drugs) are, then, variously classified. The first classification is according to taste: sweet, sour, salty, pungent, bitter or astringent. And each taste comprises two bhutas; for example, sweet foods like rice, milk, wheat are comprised of earth and water, while sour foods like yoghurt, lemon, tamarind are comprised of earth and fire.

The second classification of food is according to its post-digestive taste, in contrast to the initial 'tongue' taste. The two may not coincide. For example, eating bananas with milk decreases the digestive fire and can give rise to colds, coughs and allergies. The two are examples of incompatible foods because although both have a sweet taste, the post-digestive taste of bananas is sour while that of milk is sweet.

The third classification is whether the food is 'heating' or 'cooling' in its action on the body—a classification that thus provides a guideline for foods that should be consumed in a particular season or at a particular time of day. Sweet, bitter and astringent tastes are generally cooling whereas sour, salty and pungent tastes are heating.

The final classification is according to the 'personality' of the food—whether a food has a purgative or a binding quality. To take an example, eating melon together with milk is not recommended. Both are sweet and cooling, yes, and thus compatible on the criteria of taste and action, yet their personalities are incompatible: milk is a laxative while melon is a diuretic.

Ayurvedic dietetics, then, is a complex matter. Its application not only requires knowledge of the various qualities of different foods but also how these qualities interact and are influenced by different seasons, climatic zones and methods of cooking. One of the ten techniques in which a traditionally trained Ayurvedic physician was expected to excel was cooking. Most Indians do not possess such expert knowledge. What they have internalized, though, are rough and ready guidelines picked up from family elders in the process of growing up. Thus, for instance, they have lists of 'hot' and 'cold' foods and thus know which foods should not be eaten during a certain season or time of day; the most common example of this would be the prohibition on the consumption of yoghurt at night. In a commonly believed linkage of foods to emotions, onions, garlic and meat are believed to increase the sexual urge; tea and chillies make the mind restless; sour foods are bad for self-control and so on. The most common, pan-Indian preoccupation with food relates to its digestion, that is, with matters of defecation. Stools are carefully observed to see whether they are soft and even a little runny. Constipation is taken infinitely more seriously in India than in the West. The inability to defecate even for a day is as bad as a minor illness, ruining the mood of the afflicted person for the rest of the day.

There is one aspect of Ayurvedic discourse on food which,

we believe, has been relatively neglected in the description of Indian social relations. Since a person is what he eats, his consciousness is not only formed by the 'consciousness' that is present in the food but also by the consciousness of the cook. This view is most developed among the Jains, as also in one of the largest of the Hindu communities, the Vaishnavas.

The strict vegetarianism of these two and other such Indian religious communities is partly dictated by the image of the extreme pain and terror of the animal while being slaughtered, a pain and terror that becomes a part of the animal's very flesh. In the West, it is only a great chef who would echo this and go so far as to allow that one can taste the emotional state of the animal one is eating. In an article in *The New Yorker* on two great chefs, Adam Gopnik quotes Fergus Henderson, famed for his devotion to meat, on the difference in muscle tension between Welsh and Yorkshire rabbits which a discerning diner can taste on his plate. 'Rabbits, when they're wild, have a very different temperament, which is expressed in their muscles. Welsh rabbits used to have a certain...tension; you could *taste* their tension. Now we've been using more relaxed Yorkshire rabbits, which are splendid in their way, but not as tense and interesting.'[8] Alain Passard, an icon of French cuisine, who famously converted to vegetarian cooking, unwittingly embraces Vaishnava food ideology when he says, '...every day I was struggling to have a creative relationship with a corpse, a dead animal! And I could feel inside me the weight and sadness of the *cuisine animale*. And since [he turned vegetarian]—gone.' He goes on to say that the switch to vegetarian cooking not only changed his digestion but also brought a new lightness of step and spirit into his life.[9]

Many Indians, of course, go even further than the great French chef's epiphany. Their dietary habits are dictated in part not only by the consciousness in the food but also of the *cook*. One of the most respected figures in Vaishnava history,

Rupa Goswami, wrote: 'If you eat food prepared by the wicked, you will become wicked.'[10] The kitchen, then, becomes one of the most important places in the house, an extension of the Vedic altar, its sanctity guarded by many taboos, such as not entering it with one's shoes (of leather) on, or not allowing into it people whose consciousness is presumed to be in a state of impurity and thus of a lower order. Even today in most well-to-do, traditional households, the cook is invariably a brahmin, whose consciousness is believed to be more evolved than that of other castes.

The 'bad' consciousness in food (even vegetables are believed to suffer when cut) is sought to be mitigated by viewing it as a preparation for the gods, the humans only consuming the 'leftovers', the prasad, after the god or goddess has been ritually fed. Even animal food becomes 'better' if it is seen as a sacrifice to the gods. All meat eaters and eaters of food prepared by those of an impure, lower consciousness—Muslims, Europeans and the lowest castes—must then be kept far away from the kitchen and the dining space so that they do not contaminate the family with their inferior consciousness. The pollution feared is not only of the body through touch but also of the mind. The lower consciousness of the lowest castes is, in turn, also related to their ingestion of 'bad' foods.

Of course, things have changed, and caste Hindus cannot afford to be as puritanical and fastidious as before. Does the explosion in the number of restaurants in large cities and towns following the economic liberalization of the 1990s then mean that the traditional ideology in relation to food is in a state of decline? The mushrooming of restaurants that serve all kinds of food and meats from various cuisines of India and the world would suggest that this is indeed the case. What has happened, however, is a modification rather than jettisoning of the traditional food ideology. We should not underestimate the Indian affinity for tradition *and* for contextualization, the latter constantly amending the former in service of pragmatic ends. Just as in the past any hand engaged in work—the carpenter's hand hammering in a nail; even the smith's, using the 'impure' leather bellows—was declared to be always ritually pure, thus avoiding severe disruptions in economic activity, the traditional food ideology no longer applies to public spaces such as restaurants, although there are certain taboos which continue to be observed. Thus it will be a very rare Hindu who will eat beef in a restaurant in India, or not feel uneasy in the company of someone eating beef at the same table. Yet contextualization can apply even to this strictest of prohibitions, as in the case of Hindus eating steak with all apparent signs of enjoyment in restaurants *outside* India, with the explanation—given sometimes in all seriousness—that it is only the Indian cow that is holy!

## HEALTH AND MODERN MEDICINE

Considering the extent to which Ayurveda shapes an Indian's ideas about the body, one would expect that Hindu patients, at least, would primarily seek treatment from Ayurvedic practitioners. But this is not the case. The number of patients who resort *exclusively* to Ayurveda is minuscule. If we exclude self-medication—the so-called grandmother's remedies consisting of herbs, spices and particular foods which may have Ayurvedic knowledge at their base—Ayurveda becomes an option only after bio-medical treatment has been tried and has proved ineffective. Studies in 'health-seeking behaviour' show that Western biomedicine enjoys widespread acceptance and an allopath may be the first point of a medical consultation. This differs, of course, according to rural–urban location, by economic status, age and gender; urban, adult male patients with higher income are more likely to consult an allopath than are the rural poor, especially if the sick person happens to be a woman or a child.[11] Yet, overall, most Indians today, if they seek medical intervention at all, will first go to an allopathic doctor. This is surprising, considering the cost and the appalling quality of biomedicine available to the rural or, for that matter, the urban poor, who still form a majority of India's population of over a billion people.

Western biomedicine in India is provided by large public and private hospitals in cities and towns, by private practitioners and by the state-run primary health centres in villages which are meant to serve the health needs of the rural poor. These last are in an abysmal state of disrepair, lacking even basic infrastructure, equipment and drugs. They are also marked by a high rate of absenteeism of health care providers who are supposed to be manning them—that is, when qualified doctors, many of whom dream of emigrating to the West, are willing to be located in rural areas in the first place. The result is that even though primary health care is notionally 'free', most people turn to private practitioners for medical care. Naturally, then, an episode of serious illness in a poor family can plunge it into abject poverty.[12]

Private medical practitioners in India span the whole range of qualified doctors trained in Western medicine, physicians trained in modern colleges of Ayurvedic and Unani medicine (who have also been taught some fundamentals of biomedicine as a part of their curriculum) and pharmacists and other partially qualified people, almost three times the number of trained doctors, who have picked up the basics of biomedicine from experience. Excepting the high-quality care available to the well-off in urban areas, much of the practice of biomedicine, even by trained doctors, consists of hurried consultations lasting barely two to three minutes. The physical examination, in the absence of diagnostic tests, seldom involves anything more than listening to the lungs, the heart and the abdomen with a stethoscope. Common to all, the trained and the untrained, is aggressive interventions and a rampant misuse of antibiotics. Thus, in an average Indian village, a trained doctor would give a two-year-old with a three-day history of cough a vitamin B complex and a gentamycin intramuscular injection—not because the doctor suspected pneumonia but as a placebo, while an experienced but untrained healer would give someone with a fever a single injection of amoxicillin and treat a lack of appetite with penicillin...[13]

Most trained medical practitioners recognize this as over prescription, especially since seventy per cent of patients come with complaints that would disappear in the natural course over time. However, they justify this practice by referring to the expectation an Indian patient has from a practitioner of biomedicine. The expectation is of receiving strong medication leading to immediate relief. Injections are a perennial favourite, politely insisted upon by patients, and many doctors prescribe them as a matter of course in over three quarters of their cases.

Here we return to Ayurveda and the Indian predilection for assimilating alien systems of thought without worrying too much about the contradictions that might crop up in such an exercise. From the patient's point of view nothing needs to change except an acknowledgement that the drugs of biomedicine are strong in the sense that the 'hot' drugs are hotter and the 'cold' drugs colder than their indigenous counterparts. The 'strength', 'heat' and 'aggressivity' of these medicines—not dissimilar to the reputed attributes of India's ex-colonial overlords and of the white races in general—is a reason why some modern Ayurvedic physicians while explaining and treating a disease in Ayurvedic terms have little compunction in prescribing or dispensing drugs derived from penicillin, sulpha or cortisone. Health and healing, then, are as much in flux today as other areas of Indian life. Depending on an individual's life history, the stage of his life and the beliefs of his social group, modern Western and traditional Indian ideas on illness and its cure coexist in varying proportions in the mind of every Indian, informing the life of the body.

## VIEW OF DEATH

In a people whose consciousness is partly shaped by their rituals and a vast storehouse of mythological images, a Hindu myth relating to death and its relation to disease is a good place to begin any discussion of mortality.

Out of the happiness of his heart, Prajapati (Brahma, the Creator) began to create our universe. Each of his creatures was unique and wonderful. The ones on earth had everlasting life. Then, one day, a sound of pain reached Prajapati's ears and a smell of something rotting assailed his nostrils. He saw that a large number of his creations on earth had become old, weak, almost lifeless, and the stink arose from their old and wasted bodies.

Prajapati closed his eyes and was lost in meditation. His forehead creased in worry, his smiling visage became an unhappy one, as if clouds had darkened a sunlit sky. Just at that moment, a shadow emerged from inside him and slowly took on a body. Soon, it was a woman, with hands folded in supplication, who stood in front of him. 'Who am I, Father? Why have I been created? What is my work?' she asked.

Prajapati replied: 'You are my daughter—Death. You have been created to do the work of destruction.'

The woman said: 'I am a woman and yet you have brought me into existence for such heartless work! My woman's heart and woman's dharma will not endure such cruelty.'

Prajapati smiled and said: 'You must. There is no other way.'

Death protested but the Lord was unbending. He disappeared. She engaged in severe *tapas* (ascetic practice) for many years, till Prajapati was forced to appear before her.

'Ask for a boon,' he said.

'Please release me from the difficult karma you have given me as my lot,' Death said.

'That is not possible,' said the Lord and returned to his abode.

Death undertook further tapas, with even harder austerities, till Brahma had to appear before her again. On seeing him, Death began sobbing uncontrollably, her tears an unstoppable stream. From this stream of sorrow terrifying images rose up one after another.

'These are diseases. They are your creations and they will be your helpers,' said Prajapati.

'But, being a woman, how will I ever be able to take away a husband from the side of his wife? How will I snatch an infant from its mother's breast? What of the sin of this heartless work?'

Prajapati gestured to her to stop. 'You are beyond sin and virtue. You will not be touched by sin. People will call you only through their own karma. Human beings will be victims of wrong conduct and bad conduct, and you will only give them release from pain, peace from storm, a new birth from an old one.'

'But,' said Death, 'when wives, sons and daughters, mothers and fathers are in the throes of grief, how will I witness those heart-rending scenes?'

The Creator then said, 'I shall take away your sight. From now on you will be blind.'

'And their weeping and wailing?' asked Death. 'The heart-wrenching cries of men and women?'

'You will also be deaf. No voice will reach your ears.'

Thus Death is blind and deaf; diseases lead her by the hand toward those people who have summoned her through their own karma. Death is blameless

Like most other major religions, Hinduism denies the finality of death and has its own detailed answer to mankind's perennial query: what comes after? Hindus are taught to regard death as the end of the physical, material body (*dehanta*), not the end of existence. Death is opposed to birth, not life. It is an interval between lives and a passage into the next life. Till the final release of *moksha* or *mukti* from the cycles of life and death, man is destined for repeated rebirths, and texts enjoin one to view death with equanimity. Life and death, tradition consoles the mourners, are not different *ontological* entities, in polar opposition to each other, but facets of a single, seemingly endless cycle. Krishna's words to a mourning Arjuna in the Bhagavad Gita, often repeated to those who are left behind, have been culturally charged with consoling power for centuries: 'For death is a certainty for him who has been born and birth a certainty for him who has died. Therefore, for what is unavoidable, thou should not grieve.'[14]

With the end of the gross, physical body, the process of rebirth and reincarnation begins. From the 'earth world' (*bhuloka*) that had been his home and the object of his senses when the person was alive, his 'soul'—consciousness without a physical body—now passes into an in-between subtle or astral world where it continues to function with complete continuity. This in-between world (*antarloka*) has three sub-divisions: heaven, hell, and an intermediate 'world of spirits' (*pretaloka*) where most souls dwell for a while before traversing either heaven or hell on their way to rebirth. Heaven and hell are not places of eternal bliss or damnation but way stations where the individual soul enjoys or suffers the consequences of its good or evil deeds. We should add that in the opinion of some (and matters relating to death and rebirth are always contentious), whether the soul will go to heaven or hell depends not only on its karmic balance but also on the dying person's state of mind and his last thoughts at the moment of death. These will have a powerful influence on the creation of his next life and will determine the place where he will be reborn.

In popular culture, for instance in brightly coloured posters displayed in bazaars and village fairs, the state of heavenly bliss where the soul consorts with gods and other higher beings does not merit much attention. In contrast, the tortures of the twenty-eight hells are depicted in lurid colours and a wealth of gory detail. The punishments for misdeeds seem to be based on the principle of *lex talionis*, the law of retaliation. 'An eye for an eye, a tooth for a tooth,' it seems, is not limited to the Old Testament but also finds place in the Hindu conception of hell. In the hell reserved for the meat eater, the animals and fowl which he consumed when alive are waiting to chew and feast on *his* flesh. In the hell for the adulterer, the sinner has to embrace a 'partner' made of red-hot iron. And the man who made his wife swallow his semen (oral sex is forbidden even in the otherwise tolerant *Kamasutra*) is cast into a sea of semen where he must survive on the gooey stuff alone.

Caste, too, follows the soul into hell, although with a reverse slant: the punishment for high-caste sinners, especially brahmins, is more severe than for those of lower castes from whom, of course, little is expected in the way of higher morality. Thus, high-caste consumers of intoxicating drinks are cast into a hell where they are forced to drink melted iron; a brahmin who had sexual relations with a woman of low caste will be thrown into a well filled with excreta, urine, blood and phlegm; while brahmins who hunted wild animals must pass through a hell where the servants of the god of death hack off their limbs one by one.

What is most striking about death in the Hindu tradition is the importance of family and family bonds even after death. Immediately after death, rites are performed every day to help the vulnerable spirit which is still hovering between earth and the in-between worlds, confused and disoriented like the loved ones it has left behind, to break all bonds with its former physical existence. On the tenth day, for instance, it is offered *pinda*s—balls of rice or flour—which symbolically reconstitute specific limbs till the astral body is completed by the thirteenth day. Moreover, periodic household rituals and sacrifices, especially at certain times of the year that are set aside for the welfare of ancestral spirits, seek to underline a continuing bond between the dead and the living. In fact, for a very long time to come, at least three generations, the family will remain actively responsible for the welfare of the dead person's soul by mitigating its suffering if in hell or by pushing it through the upper reaches of heaven toward rebirth and, ultimately, toward moksha—release from the cycle of birth and death.

In conclusion, our observations on the body, health and Ayurvedic healing in India further elucidate, as they emphasize, some fundamental qualities of the Indian mind which we shall elaborate upon in the concluding chapter. The mental representation of our body—the body image, a basic element of the psyche with which we 'see' the world—is as much cultural as it is individual. The body, then, is vital in forming our view of the world and our place in it. Here, the Indian body, less differentiated from the environment and engaged in a ceaseless transaction with it, differs from a sharply bounded Western body. An average person in the West takes the primacy of inner, biological processes in health and healing for granted. The average Indian, due to the Ayurveda-inspired view of the body having a basic material identity with the environment, tends to take a more transactional view of health. In other words, whereas a consequence of the Western body image is to see sickness as something foreign and 'poisonous' *inside* the body (bacteria, virus, etc.) that needs to be rooted out, the traditional Indian view regards ill-health as a disturbance of harmony *between* the body and its environment that needs to be corrected and balance restored.

As far as death is concerned, Hinduism does not hold out the consolation of St Paul's promise that at the moment of death we will come face to face with god, and that then 'shall we know even as we are known'. Instead, it seeks to mitigate the universal dread of death by viewing it as an interval between lives, not as an end to the often painful, sometimes happy, but always engrossing and, above all, *familiar* life-in-the-world. In the words of an old Punjabi woman, as reported by the anthropologist Veena Das, death is 'like being shifted from one breast to the other breast of the mother. The child feels lost in that one instant, but not for long.'[15]

# RELIGIOUS AND SPIRITUAL LIFE

$\mathcal{I}$t is often said that Indians have an intuitive relationship with the Divine. Outwardly, he may be indistinguishable from any other trendy 'citizen of the world' but even the most modern Indian's inner terrain is liable to be imbued with a matter-of-fact religiosity. Visits to important temples and pilgrimage places, regular ritual fasting and turning to traditional religious practices or gurus have not declined with globalization and its worldly temptations. In fact, these have increased since the 1980s, and most conspicuously in the growing, new middle class.

Hinduism (and this chapter is exclusively concerned with the faith of the majority) has been shaped by many cross-currents throughout its long history. Over the centuries, the interaction and synthesis of these currents of belief has resulted in contemporary Hinduism with its varied teachings and diverse cults. 'Belief in stones and trees having souls (Animism, Pantheism) exists side by side with the belief in higher gods, the monotheistic worship of one god is as much possible as the polytheistic or demonical adoration of many gods, demons and spirits,' writes the Indologist Axel Michaels. He continues, 'The religion is lived through ritualistic (Brahminism, Tantrism), devotional (Bhakti), spiritual-mystic (asceticism, Yoga, meditation) and heroic forms...And yet to a large extent all these forms are peacefully practiced beside each other. One can almost say that religious post-modernism has been realized in India: "Anything goes".[1]

Here, we are not concerned with describing the various manifestations of Hindu religiosity. Instead, we seek to understand the influence of modernity on the contemporary religious imagination, and the religious responses to the powerful processes of social transformation. Our interest, therefore, is on current developments, such as a rapidly growing Hindu nationalism and the changing religious practices of the urban middle class where it is not religion *per se* but old religious norms and values which are losing their old verities and must be renegotiated and invested with new meaning. In the following pages, we will talk of two important actors on the contemporary religious scene—the 'Hindu nationalist' and the 'flexible Hindu'—and their varied responses to the challenges of modernity and globalization.

## THE HINDU NATIONALIST

In searching for alternative modes of life as a response to the disruptions of modernity, the reformulation of Hinduism is being strongly influenced by a nationalist, religious activism.[2] The Hindu nationalists we are talking of belong to the 'Sangh parivar'. This is a more or less loosely knit system of political, social, cultural and religious formations revolving around the Rashtriya Swayamsevak Sangh (RSS) which provides them with much of their ideological light and activist heat. Tracing its origins to the nineteenth-century reform movements within Hinduism, such as the Arya Samaj, which were born out of a resistance to European cultural domination and the Christian missionary offensive, Hindu nationalism began to gather impetus in the 1920s with the founding of the RSS.[3] But the period in which it expanded most rapidly was in the late 1980s and 1990s, the era of India's economic liberalization and the beginning of the country's integration with a global economy. In other words, the onset of globalization coincided with the explosion of Hindu nationalism.

The Hindu nationalist is attempting to confront the processes of modernization and changes in family structure with a new articulation of Hindu values and norms. For one, his is the call to keep the Hindu family atmosphere free of all cultural pollution. Since he believes the ongoing invasion of Indian cultural space by Western values is a conspiracy by forces determined to weaken India by uprooting it from its traditions, the Hindu nationalist reacts by seeking to build a united front against the cultural assault of globalization from within the family. In this defensive mobilization, the primary role assigned to the woman is that of a carrier and mediator of tradition while the man's role is that of the provider and protector.

In addition, the Hindu nationalist seeks to reformulate religious beliefs by assigning central importance to two aspects: *Ramabhakti* and *deshbhakti*, devotion to Lord Rama and devotion to the nation. The first has as its goal the elevation of Lord Rama as the central and highest Hindu divinity, while deshbhakti foregrounds the loyalty towards 'Mother India' (*Bharatmata*). Both have the ultimate goal of welding together a Hindu society that is fragmented in castes, sects and local traditions so as to prepare it to meet the challenges of globalization.

Media and modern technologies have not played an unimportant part in the realization of these objectives. The nationalist's desired homogenization of Hindu religious traditions has been propelled by the global communications revolution, especially the wide diffusion of television and now the Internet. Television, for instance, that had become a truly mass medium by the end of the 1980s, presented not only a vision of a soon-attainable consumerist heaven in its advertising spots but also a series of 'mythologicals'. The weekly broadcasts of the enormously popular serial *Ramayana*, for instance, first broadcast on the national network in 1987 to record audiences, harked back to a past golden age and defined the Hindu nationalist view of what was the essence of Indian culture. The television broadcast of the Ramanand Sagar version of the *Ramayana* not only raised Lord Rama to a pan-Indian integration figure but also played a major role in relegating the many regional traditions of the epic to the sidelines while privileging a version very close to the Hindu nationalist's heart.

Today, at the beginning of the twenty-first century, Hindu nationalism, with its proclivity to homogenize the wide variety of myths and symbols deriving from the multifarious world of Hindu gods and goddesses has become a major force on the Indian political and cultural scene. Its religious arm, the Vishwa Hindu Parishad (VHP), which has the task of providing the integrative framework—the cultural foundation—for a new unity and solidarity among the Hindus, is trying hard to project itself as the premier if not sole representative of Hindus all over the world.

The VHP's own ideology has been decisively influenced by the writings of V.D. Savarkar (1883–1966) who coined the term Hindutva ('Hindu-ness') that made a clear distinction between Hinduism as a religion—Hindu dharma—and Hindutva as a social-political force which seeks to mobilize all Hindus against foreign religious and cultural influences.[4] Defining a Hindu as one whose faith originated within the borders of an undivided India (this includes the Buddhists, Jains and Sikhs but excludes Christians and Muslims), the VHP has as one of its goals the fostering of a united Hindu nation through an institutionalized collaboration between Hindu religious leaders and Hindu nationalist activists. Here, it is the missionary activity of Christian and Islamic religious institutions that is a special object of the Hindu nationalist's ire since he believes that conversions undermine nationalism. The VHP's opposition, however, though primarily couched in the militant discourse of Hindutva, also incorporates an appeal to Hindu religious sentiment. Thus, for instance, alluding to the consumption of beef by Christians and Muslims, the VHP distributed a series of leaflets at the Maha Kumbh, a gathering of thirty to forty million pilgrims on the bank of the Ganga at Allahabad, in January 2001, where one of the leaflets stated that by stopping one conversion a Hindu could save five cows.[5] According to the VHP, conversion activity must be strenuously opposed since it destroys peace in Hindu society, 'turning brother against brother', and results in violent agitation by the converted population, such as by the Christians in north-eastern India, for separate states of their own. In a joint declaration at the 2001 Maha Kumbh, the VHP succeeded in enlisting the support of influential Hindu religious leaders, as also of the Dalai Lama, in opposing conversion by any religious tradition.

Many in India, Hindus and others, regard the VHP as a fundamentalist organization which seriously distorts traditional Hinduism. Indeed, in its efforts to define an essential Hindu identity by privileging a mythology centred on the figure of a militant Lord Rama and distilling a small number of key doctrines and practices from the remarkably diverse Hindu traditions, the VHP is slowly making the division of Hinduism into various *sampradayas* (sects) obsolete. Traditional Hindu religious leaders now routinely talk of a Hindu dharma rather than of Vaishnavism or Shaivism, to mention just the two largest Hindu sects, each with several hundred million followers.

The Hindu nationalist, then, whether a member of the RSS, VHP, Bajrang Dal or the Bharatiya Janata Party (BJP), champions homogeneity and a singular identity. He is governed by deeply conservative notions of social and family life. In his fear of a cultural alienation, especially through missionary religions and the onslaught of a cultural and economic globalization, he may be combative in spreading his ideology of a strong Hindu nation. Yet the militancy of his outlook and actions is also constrained by two binding elements of Hindu religion and culture: the themes of tolerance and universality. He is not free from these fundamental aspects of his religious-cultural identity that are also the major themes running through the *grand recit*, the 'master narrative', of Hinduism's encounter with other religions, secular ideologies and historical forces of change.

The first, the 'Hindu tolerance' theme, emphasizes Hinduism's willingness throughout history to negotiate other worldviews and accept changes without sacrificing an unchanging, essential core. The other major theme, that of Hinduism's 'universality', is somewhat different from the 'universalism' claim of other major religions. Universality for the Hindu is the conviction that the fundamental insights of his faith also lie at the heart of all other religions. In other words, the 'foreign belief' is ultimately always a part of one's own. Both these themes, as we shall see below, have consequences for the nationalist's actions. They do not in any manner lessen the propensity for extreme violence that he shares with the fundamentalists of all religions, but they can weaken the singular conviction underlying his violent acts.

In the Hindu nationalist discourse, the militancy of Hindutva is often in conflict with Hinduism's master narrative. The nationalist often seems split between a vigorous opposition to all foreign influences—proselytizing religions, cultural and economic globalization—which undermine the roots of Hindu *samaj* (society) and the tolerance ethic enjoined by the Hindu dharma. In its current phase, Hindu nationalism appears to be steering closer to the shores of militancy than of tolerance, but the latter, as we shall see later, continues to preclude an unambiguous commitment to the former. Even the founding document of the VHP must perforce take a bow towards openness: 'Hindu society today faces challenges and problems of vast magnitude, grim and intensely complex in character. But challenges and problems, vilification and vicissitudes, shocks and suppression, are not new to Hindu society...History stands as an eloquent testimony that Hindu samaj has never been unwilling or allergic to readjustment of its outer behaviour, without sacrificing its soul and spirit...'[6] The VHP ideologues may violently oppose conversions but are careful to point out—in their public statements, however unconvincing—that this opposition is only against conversions that take place because of financial enticements and other 'underhand tactics' used by the missionaries of other religions, primarily Christianity and Islam, and that they are not against an individual's free choice of another faith. In spite of many deviations in his activist and sometimes violent practice, the nationalist is unable to completely and openly renounce the ideal of tolerance expressed in Gandhi's well-known words which he often quotes with approval: 'I do not want my house to be walled on all sides and its windows to be stuffed. I want the cultures of all lands to be blown about my house as freely as possible. But I refuse to be blown off my feet by any.'[7]

Although Hindu nationalist discourse is rich in images of an embattled faith that has survived many onslaughts and endured in the face of many storms—from militant Islam to proselytizing Christianity—it is hesitant to view the current encounter with the forces of globalization solely as a confrontation. The tolerance theme of Hinduism's master narrative prevents the nationalist from articulating his response to globalization in terms of winners and losers locked in mortal combat and thus obscuring the processes of assimilation, transformation, reassertion and re-creation which, as the historian Raymond Grew notes, are characteristic of all cultural encounters.[8] Besides giving the nationalist a new self-confidence, these processes have also provided him with a forum for pursuing his interests and propagating his ideology. In other words, the nationalist's hostility toward globalization is mitigated by the fact that he regards it as a second modernization which not only holds a threat but also provides an opportunity for Hindus to actively participate in shaping its future course.

The Hindu nationalist may have had some success in eroding the importance of traditional doctrinal and liturgical concerns that led to Hinduism's division into sects, but he has not yet quite altered the mindset of the *traditionalist*—who still forms the majority of all Hindus—at least as far as his response to the challenges emanating from the outside world are concerned. Reacting within the framework of the master narrative, the traditionalist is less inclined than the nationalist to feel defensive or to take up an ideologically committed, activist stance. The Hindu tolerance theme of the narrative casts a longer shadow on the reactions of the traditionalist. Thus, for instance, whereas Jesus Christ may sometimes find mention as a figure worthy of emulation and respect in nationalist writings (a courtesy not extended to Prophet Mohammed), traditional Vaishnava gurus have little difficulty in transforming him into a son of Krishna, to give him the status of an *avatar* (incarnation of Vishnu), or to illustrate their teachings with examples from the Gospel and the lives of Christian saints.[9] But greater tolerance tends to go together with greater indifference and the Hindu traditionalist, in contrast to the nationalist, is much less concerned with the impact of globalization on his faith, tending to regard this issue, if he at all considers it worthy of his attention, as one concerned with finding 'Western answers for Western questions.'

The second major theme of Hinduism—universality—makes the Hindu nationalist hope that his religion will reign supreme in a globalized world that is being currently born and thus hinders him from walling himself off completely from foreign influences even as he combats them. To the nationalist, Hinduism is universal because its cornerstone is an eternal mystical truth, the fundamental unity of all creation, animate and inanimate. It is the recognition that the Supreme Soul pervades one and all. If all religions are different paths to the same truth—'*Ekam sat, viprah bahudda vadanti*' (One truth, many ways of reaching it)—then other religions are only different manifestations of Hinduism. At their core, then, all religions of the world are Hindu and the nationalist accepts religious pluralism because it is pluralism in appearance only.

To reach the higher states of spiritual evolution, though, the nationalist argues, one needs to go beyond appearance. Hindu pluralism does not exclude the existence of a hierarchy among the various faiths; there are many ways, yes, but not all of them are equal. In asserting that the Hindu's mystical path is a superior one for the mature individual, what we have in nationalist discourse is a tolerance of the elite for the 'lower orders', coupled with the hope that Hindu universality will be the religion of a future, more evolved world order. For the nationalist, then, globalization is not only a danger but also a unique opportunity for the Hindu ethos to establish itself as the universal ethical value system of mankind. K.S. Sudarshan, for a long time the chief ideologue of the RSS and now its head, is convinced that in the coming years 'Hindutva would dawn upon the world as the supreme philosophy and way of life'[10] where 'the belief in the ultimate victory of Hindu thought is based not on blind faith but on a deep inner awareness that Hindu philosophy is based on laws which are not just Hindu laws but universal laws applicable to all.'[11]

Although the theme of its universality is uncontested within Hinduism, the nationalist, as compared to the traditionalist and the flexible Hindu, expresses a disquiet with some of its consequences. He worries whether in placing so much emphasis on universality, on the Vedic dictum of '*Vasudhaiva kutumbakam*' (the universe is one family), the Hindus have not sacrificed the possibility of a community feeling and a necessary unity which they have lacked in the past and which they need to face the challenge of other faiths. He is concerned whether the concept of '*Vishvabandhutva*' (universal brotherhood) has not led to a weakening of '*Deshbandhutva*' (national brotherhood) and '*Dharmabandhutva*' (religious brotherhood).[12] In other words, there are two conflicting souls, of universality and nationalism, of Hindu dharma tolerance and Hindutva militancy, that are struggling within the Hindu nationalist's breast.

In the end, though, however it is interpreted by the nationalist and the traditionalist, the universality theme of Hinduism's master narrative can be problematic. Even by accepting other religious traditions as valid, as pointing to the same truth, from the vantage point of the higher 'universal' wisdom of Hinduism (and not in terms of their own self-characterization), Hindus—nationalist and others—may ultimately be hindering a dialogue with other faiths and the possible evolution of a universal ethics. In the long run, discerning a common Vedantic monism in all other religions leads not to harmony and friendship but to misunderstanding and possible discord. In one of the legends about the child Krishna, Yashoda opens the god's mouth and sees the world of Hindu cosmology within. This is the master narrative of Hinduism, with all good intentions, identifying itself with the universe of all faiths, and when this vision becomes the nationalist's expectation of a coming triumph of the Hindu worldview in a globalized world, it is fated for disappointment. Illusions, irrespective of their worth in mobilizing large numbers of peoples or creating utopian communities, ultimately remain mere illusions.

## THE FLEXIBLE HINDU

Besides the nationalist, there is another, 'flexible' Hindu—urban, educated in the modern idiom and belonging to the expanding middle class. The flexible Hindu can be a traditionalist in the sense of choosing to adopt or revive selected Hindu rituals in his religious life. He can be a nationalist in his sympathy with certain stances of the Hindu right (more VHP than RSS). And he can also—at the upper end of the socio-economic scale—be a globalist who enthusiastically embraces new religious and spiritual movements irrespective of their territorial origins. The flexible Hindu differs from the other two in that he is more eclectic in his religious attitudes and beliefs than the traditionalist and is less ideologically committed than the nationalist.

The flexible Hindu views religious occasions and rituals as important expressions of his identity.[13] Domestic rituals and fasts (*vratas*), celebration of festivals and visits to pilgrimage places are welcomed, and not only because they provide a change from the routine of daily life. The changing circumstances of urban middle-class life, however, do not allow him to do any of these things in the traditional manner. The scramble of big-city life, the increasing number of women joining the workforce or living in smaller families without the helping hands of many women, have all led to the modernization of rituals and shortening of religious ceremonies. The flexible Hindu welcomes these—often creative—alterations as he seeks to adjust traditional rituals to his changed life circumstances. Thus, for instance, the traditional frame of *karva chauth*, an annual fast undertaken by North Indian women for the health and long life of their husbands, has been progressively loosened. A young woman, concerned with her physical fitness, spoke of *karva chauth* as a welcome day of dieting. Other women, who no longer strictly observe the vow of not eating or drinking from sunrise till the moon is sighted at night, meet with friends or relatives on this day to play cards, watch television or go to the movies. They are rarely to be found in the kitchen, hungry and thirsty, preparing the evening's festive meal. Instead, they are seen with groups of friends in the gaily adorned markets or in beauty salons, and they let themselves be taken out for dinner to restaurants by their husbands.

This increasing orientation toward one's own needs rather than traditional mores is deplored by some who see in this behaviour a consumption-driven addiction to pleasure. In general, though (and this leads us back to the tolerance theme of the *grand recit*), changes in rituals and the cutting short of religious ceremonies are regarded with indulgence. As any average Hindu will concede, it is the inner stance—the bhakti and the faith—that is decisive rather than following a set of rules laid out by the elders.

A similar development has taken place with regard to pilgrimages. It is modernity that has turned religious pilgrimages into a mass phenomenon. Greater mobility, more money and regular hours of work make it possible for the flexible Hindu to seek out touristy pilgrimage destinations on weekend family outings or vacations. The interest in pilgrimages is not limited to the older generation; even youths and young adults go on pilgrimages with family or friends, linking the pleasures of community and leisure time to religious goals.

Hindu pilgrimages, *tirtha-yatra*s, have a different atmosphere from the ones found in their traditional Christian counterparts—though there is considerable similarity when we look at many Islamic, especially Sufi shrines in the subcontinent. The fourteen-kilometre long climb to one of the most popular pilgrimage sites in North India, the caves of Vaishno Devi, has a number of rain-and-snow shelters, modern toilets, refreshment stands, souvenir shops all along the way, as also horses at regular intervals that tired pilgrims can ride up to the caves. There are pilgrims who walk the entire way barefoot, surrendering themselves completely to the benevolence of the deity. There are others for whom the touristy enjoyment and companionship aspects of the pilgrimage are the decisive motivations. The noise, loud music and incredible bustle convey the feeling of being a participant in a lively annual fair. To put it differently, a pilgrimage—like a vrata or a religious festival—may well become a sensuous and pleasurable experience as long as the 'purity of heart' and the sincerity of religious feelings are not absent.

Vaishno Devi and other such deities offer themselves as objects of reverence who may occasionally severely test the devotion of their worshippers but are always available and in crisis situations intervene in the devotee's fate with miracles. If the deity fulfils the devotee's wish—mostly it has to do with the circumstances of his material life such as professional success or recovery from grave illness—then the devotee is obliged to give the money, gold or silver ornaments or symbolic sacrifice that he had promised the deity when making his wish. Little wonder that in today's India, where the growing middle class has much more money at its disposal than was the case in earlier decades, temples are 'big business.' The Tirupati Venkateshwara temple in Andhra Pradesh, one of the richest religious institutions after the Vatican, has a daily income of almost two crores of rupees—over 400,000 US dollars—from donations. The trend is not confined only to Hindu shrines. The Golden Temple, the holiest of Sikh shrines, has doubled its takings in the last ten years to a daily income of nearly one and a half crores, or 300,000 US dollars. Christian churches and Muslim shrines such as Haji Ali in Mumbai also contribute to the total yearly income of Indian gods and saints of approximately rupees eleven thousand crores, or 250 million dollars.

More than any other kind of Indian, it is the flexible Hindu who lets gods and gurus participate in his prosperity.

He offers puja, both at home and in temples, but also online, on the websites of some of the holiest temples. He uses the Internet for astrological advice on the auspicious time for his pujas and to find recipes for festive meals for specific religious occasions. *He* is the targeted visitor for the upcoming theme parks on Hindu gods and goddesses—Ramaland, Durgaland, Gangaland, that are being built on the model of Disneyland—and the intended customer for the devotional music cassettes and CDs which have captured over a third of the Indian music market.

The spread of new media and technologies—Internet, mythological comics, TV serials—is not only leading to greater homogenization of Hindu rituals and festivals but is also the main source of religious knowledge for the younger generation. On a number of TV channels, charismatic TV-gurus such as Asha Ram Bapu daily recite and comment on passages from the holy books and, in the process, like American television evangelists, are building religion-based empires with a following that is predominantly middle-class. And with a daily television 'consumption' of at least two to three hours, it is the middle-class housewife who is most susceptible to media-based religiosity.

Charismatic television gurus, healers and 'god-men' fit in seamlessly with the bhakti religiosity of the urban middle class where, similar to the Protestant faith, the individual communication with and personal relationship to the Divine are at the centre of religious awareness. A striking feature of contemporary religious developments is the ever-increasing popularity of healing-gurus, such as Sathya Sai Baba or Mata Nirmala Devi. The contemplative, meditative gurus identified with the Upanishadic tradition—such as the late Ramana Maharishi—are no longer the icons of the spiritual life among the upper and middle classes as they were for earlier generations. The flexible Hindu of today prefers gurus and religious practices that promise greater, immediate and quantifiable spiritual returns for smaller investments of time.

Gurus such as Sathya Sai Baba or Sri Sri Ravi Shankar are better attuned to the religious feeling of the flexible Hindu since they, too, orient themselves on the two great themes of Hinduism's *grand recit*: tolerance and universality. The Sathya Sai Baba movement—one of the largest religious movements of present times—fuses religious style elements from varied traditions in a wild eclecticism. [14] Sai Baba, avatara, healer and god, all at the same time, teaches a step-by-step way to salvation that resembles a simplified Vedantic 'Realization of god through a realization of the Self'. In the spirit of post-modernism, aspects of Shaivism, Vaishnavism, Shaktism and Christianity are reinterpreted and declared to be a new universalism whereby within the movement one does not speak of a new creed but of the universal validity of the guru's teachings. This claim to universality which we also encountered in the case of the Hindu nationalist is articulated in the symbol of the Sathya Sai Baba community: a five-petalled lotus which has the Hindu Om, the Christian cross, the Zoroastrian fire emblem, the Buddhist wheel and the Islamic crescent and star depicted on its petals.

'New Age' practices, which have met an enthusiastic reception in the Indian middle class since the 1990s, are similar to the Sai Baba and other new religious movements, in that they are exemplary for a postmodern religiosity which seems to have been anticipated in Hindu relativism and inclusivity. The flexible Hindu has no difficulty in integrating New Age practices in his daily life since they neither demand a break nor an alienation from his religious tradition. With the entry of New Age in the metropolises of Mumbai, Delhi or Bangalore, it is not only the practices of Reiki, Pranic Healing, Lama Fera, Tarot or Feng Shui but also Indian cultural concepts—for instance, the idea of karma—that are being reimported in their

Western reincarnations. Courses on coping with stress that incorporate meditation or Yoga are as much a part of the menu as astrology, aromatherapy, Egyptian Tarot, aura readings, magnetic healing or channeling.

However, irrespective of how Westernized a flexible Hindu may be, his weekend or package-tour pilgrimages, his turning to gurus, keeping fasts or integrating New Age practices in his life all connect him to tradition and affirm his Hindu identity. In other words, the flexible Hindu's response to modernity is not a turning away from his religious heritage but giving it a new form and adapting it to his changed life circumstances.

The Hindu nationalist may be disapproving of the flexible Hindu, tending to regard him with suspicion as the Indian outpost of globalization. He may belittle the flexible Hindu's religiosity as carnivalesque, look down on him as someone who promiscuously adorns himself with religious stylistic scraps from all parts of the world and thus 'weakens' the Hindu faith and dilutes Indian identity. Yet, constrained by the narrative of Hindu openness and tolerance, he cannot exclude the flexible Hindu from the Hindu fold. Such an exclusion would also be a betrayal of one of Hindu nationalism's greatest icons, the activist monk Swami Vivekananda, who wrote: 'We not only tolerate but we Hindus accept every religion, praying in the mosque of the Mohammedans, worshipping before the fire of Zoroastrians and kneeling before the cross of the Christians, knowing that all the religions, from the lowest fetishism, mean so many attempts of the human soul to grasp and realize the infinite, each determined by the conditions of its birth and association.'[15]

In spite of the differences, the coming together of the Hindu nationalist religious ideals with the values of the emerging middle class has been often commented upon. Indeed, the flexible Hindu identifies with many of the religious-cultural values of the nationalist such as a fear of Western cultural domination and the danger posed by an aggressive Muslim-Arabic world. It is unimportant whether these fears are historically or otherwise justified. The worry about a decay of ancient cultural values and a diffuse feeling of vulnerability to foreign domination are sufficient for many Hindus to turn to political parties and organizations that promise an alternative modernity, a modernity in which Hindus can embrace modern global markets, technologies and lifestyles without giving up their Hindu identity, or their sense of Hinduism being the mother religion, superior to all others.

The flexible Hindu, however, is also, almost unwittingly, the biggest inner enemy of the Hindu nationalist movement. He is the Pied Piper to a whole generation. Firmly entrenched in the establishment, this English-speaking, opinion-making segment of Indian society is the ominous concretization of an otherwise abstract global threat. He is a threat to the Hindu nationalist because of his receptiveness to the liberal, indeed 'licentious' Western sexual attitudes and mores imported into Hindu homes through television programmes and advertisements, such as those for clothes and bodily care that excite prurient interest. The protest against the ubiquity, significance and manifestations of the sexual self, so central to Western artistic and literary discourse of the twentieth century, has been basic to both conservative and fundamentalist rhetoric in many parts of the world, and the Hindu nationalist, too, reacts violently against its 'cultural pollution'. Whether protesting against beauty contests or denouncing the freer comingling of the sexes, the nationalist condemns all manifestations of modernity which arouse the senses instead of calming them, which stoke the sensual fire instead of dousing its flames. Equating globalization with consumerism and cynicism toward such traditional Hindu values as restraint on the satisfaction of material and sensual desires, and locating its threat in the flexible Hindu within the country, the nationalist solution is pithily stated by Swami Chinmayananda, a founder of the VHP: 'Let us convert Hindus to Hinduism and then everything would be all right.' This is the nationalist's battle cry in the current contention over Hindu religious identity and a task that, ironically, requires 'missionary zeal'[16] on the part of the Hindu nationalist.

In short, the Hindu nationalist and the flexible Hindu are cousins with a common family heritage. They are, however, also often adversaries, with the nationalist chafing against the restraints imposed by the *grand recit* of traditional Hinduism, while the flexible Hindu revels in the freedom it grants him to explore the spiritual byways and materially beneficial constructs of other traditions. There is no sign that the tension between the two will disappear any time in the near future.

# CONFLICT: HINDUS AND MUSLIMS

𝓘n the year 1924, writing on the causes of Hindu–Muslim conflict, Mahatma Gandhi observed, 'I see no way of achieving anything in this afflicted country without a lasting heart unity between Hindus and Mussalmans...There is no question more important and more pressing than this. In my opinion, it blocks all progress.'[1]

Gandhi's observation on the importance of finding a solution to the conflict for India's future integrity and well-being continues to be valid, although he may not have sufficiently appreciated that what appears to be a perennial conflict between India's two largest communities is not about religion. That is, it is not about matters of religious belief, dogmas, worship or adherence to different faiths and gods. Most knowledgeable commentators have identified factors other than religion as the root cause of an ostensibly religious conflict. Yet while there is near unanimity on the conflict not being religious, there is a singular lack of agreement on its root cause.[2]

Historically-minded Hindu nationalists, politically represented by one of India's two largest political parties, the Bharatiya Janata Party (BJP), view the conflict in civilizational terms. They see Hindu–Muslim relations framed by the fundamental divide of a thousand-year-old conflict between two civilizations in which the Muslims, militarily victorious and politically ascendant for centuries, tried to impose Islam on their Hindu subjects through all means, from coercion to bribery and cajolery, and yet had only limited success.[3] In the Hindu nationalists' view, the vast majority of Hindus kept their civilizational core intact while they resentfully tolerated the Muslim onslaught. The rage of the denigrated Hindu, stored up over long periods of time, had to explode once historical circumstances sanctioned such eruptions.

Other historians, of a more liberal or indeed of a leftist bent, belonging to the 'secular' school, aver that Hindus and Muslims are relatively recent categories in Indian history.[4] In precolonial and early colonial times, there was a comingling of Hindus and Muslims, most of them converted Hindus in any case. Persian and Turkish elements were incorporated into Indian society and there was a flowering of a composite cultural tradition, not only in music, art and architecture but also in the development of a syncretic popular religion. According to liberal historians, the large-scale violence between the two communities, which began to spread in the late nineteenth century, was chiefly because of colonialism, namely the British policy of deliberately strengthening Muslim identity because of the threat of Indian nationalism in which Hindus played a prominent part.[5] Nevertheless, the composite culture shared by Hindus and Muslims is still alive, especially in rural India, and comes under strain because of the need of political parties to polarize Hindu and Muslim identities for electoral gains.

In contrast to the historians of either camp, ordinary Indians operate with both versions of history. In times of heightened conflict between the two communities, the Hindu nationalist history that supports the version of age-old animosity between the two assumes pre-eminence and organizes cultural memory in one particular direction. In times of relative peace, the focus shifts back to the secular history that emphasizes commonalities and shared pieces of the past. Many of the cultural memories that were appropriate during the conflict will retreat, fade or take on new meaning, while others that incorporate the peaceful coexistence of Hindus and Muslims will resurface.

Then there are those, mostly of a Marxist persuasion, who accord primacy to the *economic* factor. The conflict between the two communities that leads to violent clashes, they believe, has less to do with religion than with 'communalism'. Communalism is a specifically Indian concept which signifies a strong identification with a community of believers based not only on religion but also common social, political and especially economic interests which conflict with the corresponding interests of another community of believers—the 'enemy'—sharing the same geographic space. In the economic vision, the 'real' cause of violence generally embraces some version of a class struggle between the poor and the rich. This, it is claimed, is as true of the anti-Semitic pogroms in fourteenth-century Spain, of sixteenth-century Catholic–Protestant violence in France and of anti-Catholic riots in nineteenth-century London,[6] as of contemporary Hindu–Muslim riots in India.

Political scientists add another dimension to this Marxist theory. They point out that Hindu–Muslim conflict, a consequence of competition for resources, may have become worse in the changed *political* context of the last sixty-odd years since the end of colonial rule. If Hindu–Muslim relations were better in the past, with much less overt violence, it was also due to the kind of polity in which the two peoples lived. This polity was that of empire, the Mughal empire followed by the British one. An empire, the political scientist Michael Walzer observes, is characterized by a mixture of repression of any strivings for independence, tolerance for different cultures, religions and ways of life, and an insistence on things remaining peaceful. It is only with the end of the empire that such political questions as 'Who *among us* shall have power here, in these villages, these towns?' or 'Which group will dominate, what will be the new ranking order?' that lead to a heightened awareness of religious-cultural differences and create the potential for violent conflict.[7] (The rise of fundamentalist groups and the politicization of religious differences in many parts of the world at the end of colonialism have been amply documented.[8]) Other political scientists, emphasizing more local than international relations, show that riots between Hindus and Muslims in India generally occur in towns and cities where formal professional and trade associations which include members of both communities are weak or non-existent.[9]

*Social psychology*, on the other hand, would emphasize the threat to identity that is being posed by the forces of modernization and globalization to peoples in many parts of the world as a root cause for Hindu–Muslim conflict. There are feelings of loss and helplessness accompanying dislocations and migrations from rural areas to the shanty towns of urban megalopolises, the disappearance of craft skills that underlay traditional work identities, and the humiliation caused by the homogenizing and hegemonizing impact of the modern world, which pronounces ancestral cultural ideals and values outmoded and irrelevant. These changes heighten the group aspects of identity as the affected—*and* afflicted—look to cultural-religious groups to help them combat their feelings of helplessness and loss and also serve as vehicles for the redress of injuries to self-esteem.

Besides the relatively sophisticated descriptions of historians, political scientists, sociologists and social psychologists on the roots of conflict, we also have the rough and ready brush strokes of the *demographic* perspective which says that urban areas, and within them only those with a Muslim minority population ranging between twenty and forty per cent of the total population, have always been prone to violence between Hindus and Muslims.[10] Presumably, with a population share of under twenty per cent, a minority is much too scared to retaliate against anything that it may perceive as a provocation. Violence, in such a situation, if it occurs at all, will have the nature of a pogrom rather than a riot.

## HINDU IMAGE OF THE MUSLIM

The dominant Hindu image of Muslims encountered in many parts of the country, and especially when tension between the communities is high, is of the *powerful* and *animal-like* Muslim. Common to the two attributes of Muslim power and animality is the Hindu conviction that a Muslim is 'naturally' aggressive and prone to violence. Although newly reinforced by the militancy in Kashmir and the spate of terrorist acts by Muslim extremists, this image goes back a long time. Mahatma Gandhi, for instance, who was assassinated by a Hindu fanatic because he was believed to have a 'soft corner' for Muslims, held the view that their young religion and imperialist expansion for thirteen centuries had made Muslims an aggressive lot.[11] Shared alike by men and women, the image of the powerful Muslim is more pronounced in men, especially when violent conflict between the communities is imminent.

This is in contrast to the Hindu self-perception of being weak, weak because divided. In interviews conducted shortly after riots in 1990 in Hyderabad, several Hindus spoke of the unity among the Muslims. 'Anything happens in a Muslim community, they all become one. We don't because of our different castes. Every caste has its own customs and life style...We are not united. Each one is engrossed in himself. The rich try to exploit the poor. This does not happen with the

Muslims. Though they have rich and poor, at least at times of prayer they are one and they all do it together at the same time. It develops unity among them. Our system is not like that. Each one goes to the temple to perform puja at his own time and in his own way and then leaves. There is no communication between us. If we could also show togetherness in our prayers, we would definitely become united and stronger than the Muslims.'

For many Hindus, the Muslim is powerful not only because he is united, but also because he is armed, favoured by the state in India, and in times of conflict supported and even armed by Pakistan. 'Muslims have a constant supply of weapons coming from Pakistan, or maybe they are locally made. They are always well-stocked. Even the poorest Muslim house will have at least a butcher's knife because they all eat meat. Hindus are not so well-equipped. If the government continues to please the Muslims and makes laws against the Hindu majority, these riots will continue forever. If processions are to be banned, both Ganesh and Muharram processions should be banned. Why is only the Ganesh procession banned? It is like blessing and protecting only one community and behaving like a stepmother toward the other.'[12]

It is interesting to note that generally a Hindu's self-identification as a Hindu occurs only when he talks of the Muslim; otherwise the conversations on his affiliation are more in terms of caste. A Hindu is born only when the Muslim enters the scene. Hindus cannot think of themselves as such without a simultaneous awareness of the Muslim's presence. This is not so for Muslims, who do not need Hindus for self-awareness. The presence of the Hindu may increase the Muslim's sense of his religious identity but does not constitute it.

The second ingredient of the Hindu image of the Muslim, as we've said earlier, is that of his *animality*. In other words, Hindus attribute to the Muslim male a physical ferocity, rampant sexuality, search for instant gratification and a dirtiness which is less a matter of bodily cleanliness and more an inner pollution that is a consequence of the consumption of forbidden, tabooed foods: 'The Muslims are good only in two things— they eat and copulate like beasts. Who else except a Muslim would even think of going to bed with his uncle's daughter, who is next to his real sister?'[13]

The above quote, from a fifty-year-old anthropological account, reflects an image of the Muslim that has remained consistent to this day. As is the following: 'Muslims always had an eye for our women. This habit persists. Good thoughts and thoughts of god come into their minds only when they shout "Allah-u-Akbar!"...They force themselves on women; they are obsessed by women and sex. Look at all the children they produce, dozens, while we are content with two or three.'[14]

Muslims are not only sexually rapacious, they are also considered dirty ('They bathe only on Fridays, the day of communal prayer in the mosque'). The ascribed dirtiness is not only a matter of personal hygiene but is more fundamental: the Muslims eat beef, an abomination for the Hindu, a more serious violation of the moral code for many than conversion to Islam or marriage to a Muslim.

The eating of beef and thus the killing of cows by Muslims has perhaps historically been the most important source of Hindu bitterness. Travelling through Tipu Sultan's dominions in the seventeenth century, Abbe Dubois tells us that though Hindus witnessed the slaughter of cows without uttering loud complaint, they were far from insensible to the insult.[15] Powerless, they contented themselves with complaining in secret and storing up in their hearts all the indignation they felt about this sacrilege. For centuries, Hindus who had been forcibly converted to Islam could not reconvert if they had eaten beef, even if under duress. The Muslim eating of beef and the Hindu abomination creates perhaps the most effective barrier against 'lasting heart unity' between the two communities that was Gandhi's ardent wish for India. It is difficult to be close to someone with whom one cannot share a meal and whose eating habits one finds disgusting.

Such images of the other community lead a stubborn existence in the deeper layers of the psyche that are impervious to rational discourse. Thus when studying the phenomena of spirit possession in rural North India, it was instructive to see that in a large number of cases, the malignant spirit possessing a Hindu man or woman was that of a Muslim. When, during the healing ritual, the patient went into a trance and the possessing spirit spoke through him, expressing its wishes, these wishes—for forbidden sexuality and prohibited foods such as meat—invariably turned out to be those that would have been horrifying to the possessed person's conscious awareness.[16] Possession by a Muslim spirit, then, seemed to reflect the afflicted person's desperate efforts to convince himself and others that his imagined transgressions and sins of the heart belonged to the 'unclean' Muslim alien and was farthest away from his 'good' Hindu self. In that Muslim spirits were universally considered to be the strongest, vilest, the most malignant and stubborn of the evil spirits, the Muslim seemed to symbolize *the* alien in the more subconscious parts of the Hindu mind.

### MUSLIM IMAGE OF THE HINDU

Besides the inevitable attribution to the 'other' of immorality and lack of control over impulses—a dirtiness of the soul— Muslims also see Hindus as a *cruel* and *cowardly* people.

'If a Hindu woman or child walks through a Muslim street, the Muslim will let them go, thinking the fight is between men and should not involve women, children and the aged. A Hindu does not think like that. It is enough for him to see the other person is a Muslim before he strikes without regard for age or gender...

'Hindus are cowards who can fight only when they are in a large group. Muslims are not afraid even if they are few and unarmed and their opponents have swords. Allah gives them courage and they know if they die the death will not be in vain but a martyrdom which Allah will reward in paradise.'[17]

Among the Muslim poor, one becomes aware of a weary resignation in their dislike of the Hindus. They tend to see themselves as helpless victims of changed historical circumstances where India, irrespective of its formal constitution, has become a Hindu country. The regime is now of the Hindus and discrimination against Muslims a fact of life. This is the striking difference between the Hindu and Muslim poor: the former feel less like victims and have a greater sense of agency and control over the circumstances of their lives than the latter. The Muslim poor give the impression of following a purposeless course, buffeted by the impact of others in a kind of social Brownian motion.

With an inchoate sense of oppression and the looming shadow of a menacing future, the besieged Muslim feels compelled to mount the battlements of his faith. In other words, he withdraws further into the shelter provided by his religious community, holding on tightly to all markers of his religious identity—the Quran, the Sharia, the Urdu language, the madrassa or religious school—which his religious leaders tell him will lead him out of his current predicament. It is only thus that he can recapture the glory that came the way of his ancestors who strictly adhered to the tenets of Islam. To him, then, the present bad condition of the Muslims, their ghettoization is not due to historical changes but because of a glaring internal fault: the 'weakening' or loss of religious faith.

'No wonder,' says one mullah, 'that Islam is bending under

the assault of *kufr* (unbelief); Arabs are bowing before Jews and Christians, you before the Hindus. What is this preoccupation with worldly wealth and success? Allah says, I did not bring you into the world to make two shops out of one, four out of two. Does the Quran want you to do that? Does the Prophet? No! They want you to dedicate yourself to the faith, give your life for the glory of Islam.'[18]

The loss of a collective self-idealization, or self-esteem, is also evident in the case of the elite among the Indian Muslims. The despair at the moral decay and political decline of Muslim societies, the historian Mushirul Hasan tells us, is a recurrent theme in Urdu literature and journalism.[19] For many, this mourning is never completed; the stock of narratives of loss and their elegiac mood, most vividly captured in the *ghazal*, is passed from one generation to the next. For these 'dispossessed' men and women of the elite classes, the sentiment expressed in the poet Iqbal's line, '*Barq girti hai to bechare Mussulmanon par*' (Lightning only strikes the hapless Muslims), has become part of their social identity. In other words, whenever such a person feels, thinks and acts like a Muslim rather than as an individual, there is an undertone of grief, a miasma of mourning in what has been called 'the Andalus syndrome'.[20] The syndrome, of course, refers to the great Muslim civilization on the Iberian Peninsula that ended abruptly in the sixteenth century, plunging the Islamic world into gloom and leaving a yearning for its lost glory in Muslim societies on the rim of the Mediterranean. For a long time, both during British rule and in an independent India with an overwhelming Hindu majority, the Andalus syndrome was a significant part of the psyche of the Muslim upper class. Now, the situation seems to be changing, in so far as the younger generation is better prepared to face the old challenges and seize the opportunities provided by modernization rather than remain in a state of perpetual mourning.

### FROM CONFLICT TO VIOLENCE

As with an individual, where the 'faultlines' of personality are most clearly visible in a state of its breakdown, the psychological dimensions of Hindu–Muslim conflict become transparent when a dormant conflict breaks out in large-scale violence. These are the 'communal riots' which have been a recurrent feature of the Indian social and political landscape.

## The build-up to violence

Leaving aside the conundrum of the 'root' cause of Hindu–Muslim violence (since all the possible causes—economic, historical, political, social-psychological, demographic—are encountered in almost every riot situation), the eruption of a riot is never unexpected and yet takes everyone by surprise. By eruption we do not mean that a riot is spontaneous and involves no degree of planning or preparation, but only that it generally takes place suddenly after a considerable degree of tension between the two communities has been built up. To change the metaphor, the riot is a bursting of a boil, the eruption of pus, of 'bad blood' between Hindus and Muslims which has accumulated over a few days or weeks in a particular location. In some cities—Ahmedabad and Hyderabad come immediately to mind—where the boil is a festering sore, the tension never disappears but remains at an uncomfortable level below violent eruption.

The build-up of immediate tension occurs when religious identities come to the forefront in a large number of people because of a perceived threat to this particular identity. The threat, a collective distortion of the meaning of a real event, makes members of the community act demonstratively through words and actions as Hindus, or as Muslims. In turn, the demonstration of this religious identity threatens members of the other community who, too, begin to mobilize their identity around their religious affiliation. Thus begins a spiral of perceived (or misperceived) threats and counter postures which raises the tension between the two communities.

In the period of tension, individuals increasingly think of themselves as Hindus or Muslims and see members of the other community as stereotypes. We have already seen these stereotypes—the Hindu and Muslim images of each other—that are attributed to the adversarial group and orally transmitted down generations. As tension mounts, all these are recalled, and there follows an inevitable homogenization and depersonalization as individual Hindus or Muslims become interchangeable. Each community perceives the other in terms of a group category rather than a collection of people with their personal, idiosyncratic natures. The individual disappears, and remarks such as 'Look what the Hindus are doing!' or 'The Muslims have crossed all limits!' increase markedly.

The conscious experiencing and expression of identity through religion rather than through other group identities such as those of family, caste or profession varies with individuals. At the one extreme there are always some Hindus and Muslims whose personal identity is not overwhelmed by their communal identity even in the worst phases of a violent conflict. These are persons who wear their group identity lightly and are capable of acts of compassion and self-sacrifice, such as saving members of the 'enemy' group from the fury of a rampaging mob even at considerable danger to their own physical safety. On the other extreme there are others—the fanatics—whose behaviour even in times of peace is dictated by their communal identity, an armour that is rarely taken off.

In both communities, communal identities also tend to be less salient for women than men, a difference that seems to be rooted in their developmental histories. In Hyderabad, where Hindu–Muslim riots are frequent, a study revealed that there was a significant difference between boys and girls between the ages of ten and fifteen when they were given the task of constructing an 'exciting' scene using toys and dolls easily identifiable as Hindu or Muslim.[21] Scenes of violence between the two communities were relatively absent in the girls' constructions, whereas they dominated those of the boys. Even when they identified the dolls as Hindu or Muslim, girls tended to construct peaceful scenes from family life, with the excitement—such as a policeman chasing a robber—banished to the periphery.

With the movement of religious identities to the forefront, one knows that any particular conflict between the two communities, generally resulting from a blend of political and economic aims or grievances, will be imbued with religious ultimacy. In other words, the involvement of religious identities will ensure that the issues at stake become life and death issues through the employment of the arsenal of powerful religious symbols and rhetoric.

## The role of religious-political demagogues

While the rhetoric of violence becomes frequent in times of tension, it still remains a substitute for action. The activation of a full-scale, violent Hindu–Muslim conflict—a riot—needs powerful additional impulses. The 'zone of indifference' with regard to one's faith and religious community in which everyday life is lived, free of excessive and obsessive scrutiny, may be breached by momentous external events such as the demolition of the Babri mosque. But the breach needs considerable widening before violence becomes possible. It is here that religious demagogues, owing allegiance to fundamentalist religious-political formations, enter the scene. On the one hand, they stoke the group's persecution anxiety with images of a besieged and endangered community on the verge of extinction at the hands of the 'enemy' group. On the other, they heighten the group's narcissism by singing of its glories while ridiculing the other community.

Let us first listen to a notorious Hindu nationalist demagogue, Sadhavi Rithambara:

> The long-suffering Hindu is being called a religious zealot today only because he wants to build a temple. The Muslims got their Pakistan. Even in a mutilated India, they have special rights. They have no use for family planning. They have their own religious schools. What do we have? An India with its arms cut off [a reference to the map of India after Partition]. An India where restrictions are placed on our festivals, where our processions are always in danger of attack, where the expression of our opinions is prohibited, where our religious beliefs are cruelly derided...
>
> In Kashmir, the Hindu was a minority and was hounded out of the valley. Slogans of 'Long live Pakistan' were carved with red-hot iron rods on the thighs of our Hindu daughters. Try to feel the unhappiness and pain of the Hindu who became a refugee in his own country. The Hindu was dishonoured in Kashmir because he was in a minority. But there is a conspiracy to make him a minority in the whole country. The state tells us Hindus to have only two or three children. After a while, they will say do not have even one. But what about those who have six wives, have thirty or thirty-five children and breed like mosquitoes and flies?...
>
> I submit to you that when the Hindu of Kashmir became a minority he came to Jammu. From Jammu he came to Delhi. But if you Hindus are on the run all over India, where will you go? Drown in the Indian Ocean or jump from the peak of the Himalayas?...[22]

The Muslim demagogue retorts with apocalyptic images: 'Awake, O Indian Muslims, before you disappear completely! Even your *story* will not find mention in other stories.'[23] Here, the demagogue can count on memories of previous Hindu–Muslim riots all over the country which have almost always had their origin in the fear of one community being exterminated or seriously damaged by the other. The demolition of the Babri mosque in 1992 played into the long-standing fear of Indian Muslims of being swamped by a preponderant and numerous Hindu host, a chain of associations leading from the razing of an unused mosque to the disappearance of Islam in India. The 1969 riot in Ahmedabad was preceded by a period of tension when the RSS, the spearhead of Hindu nationalism, began a campaign demanding the 'Indianization' of Muslims and thus initiating a similar chain of mental associations.

For the Hindus, the Muslim threat is to the very survival of their homeland; India is imperilled either through the Muslim's identification with pan-Islamic causes or in the demand for a separate cultural identity, expressed through the insistence on maintaining Islamic personal law or in demanding a greater role for Urdu. Here the threat to the Hindus travels through an associative chain where such Muslim demands are viewed as precursors to violent Muslim separatism (as in Kashmir), the creation of another Pakistan and, ultimately, the dreaded revival of medieval Muslim rule.

As in individuals, where persecution anxiety often manifests itself in threats to the integrity of the body, especially during psychotic episodes, the speech of the demagogues is rich in metaphors of the 'community-body' under concrete, physical assault. The imagery of the Hindu or Muslim body amputated, raped, slashed, harnesses the power of unconscious fantasy to amplify the threat of persecution, anchoring the dubious *logos* of a particular political argument deeply in the popular imagination through the power of *mythos*.

To Gandhi's cherished dream of 'lasting heart unity' between Hindus and Muslims, Sadhavi Rithambara's response is this:

> They ask what would happen to Muslims in a Hindu India.
> I tell them Muslims will not be dishonoured in a Hindu state nor will they be rewarded to get their votes. No umbrella

will open in Indian streets because it is raining in Pakistan. If there is war in the Gulf then slogans of 'Long live Saddam Hussein' won't be shouted on Indian streets. And as for unity with our Muslim brothers, we say, 'Brother, we are willing to eat *sevian* at your house to celebrate Eid but you don't want to play with colours with us on Holi. We hear your calls to prayer along with our temple bells, but you object to our bells. How can unity ever come about? The Hindu faces this way [when praying], the Muslim the other. The Hindu writes from left to right, the Muslim from right to left. The Hindu prays to the rising sun, the Muslim faces the setting sun when praying. If the Hindu eats with the right hand, the Muslim with the left. If the Hindu calls India 'Mother', she becomes a witch for the Muslim. The Hindu worships the cow, the Muslim attains paradise by eating beef. The Hindu keeps a moustache, the Muslim always shaves the upper lip. Whatever the Hindu does, it is the Muslim's religion to do the opposite. I say, 'If you want to do everything contrary to the Hindu, then the Hindu eats with his mouth; you should do the opposite in this matter too!'[24]

The vision of the Muslim fundamentalist—Ubedullah Khan Azmi in this case—too, is of Hindus and Muslims in eternal competition. Here, for example, is his view on which community is more civilized, stronger and generally better:

It was the believers in the Quran who taught you [Hindus] the graces of life, taught you how to eat and drink. All you had before us were tomatoes and potatoes. What did you have? We brought jasmine, we brought frangipani. We gave the Taj Mahal, we gave the Red Fort. India was made India by us. We lived here for eight hundred years and we made India shine. In thirty-five years you have dimmed its light and ruined the country. A beggar will not be grateful if made an emperor. Lay out a feast for him and he will not like it. Throw him a piece of bread in the dust and he will get his appetite back. Do not force us to speak. Do not force us to come in front of you as an enemy. God, look at their ignorance to believe we have no words when out of pity we gave them the power of speech.[25]

Azmi's attempt to sharply differentiate Hindus from Muslims, suggesting that Muslims consider themselves as having come to India from outside the country eight hundred years ago (and from a superior racial stock) can be seen as a consequence of the heightened antagonism between the two communities on the eve of a riot. In such a situation, the fundamentalist exhorts the Muslims to shun contamination by any of the Hindu symbols and strive to keep their shared Islamic identity intact and pure. You should regularly say your prayers, he continues, keep your fasts even in the heat of summer. Give your life a religious cast. Live according to the Quran and then you are bound to be victorious: 'We have passed under arches of swords. We have come through the battlefield of Karbala. We have passed through the valleys of Spain, through the hills of Gibraltar, through the plains of India. We can say with pride that in spite of thousands of ordeals it has undergone, the Muslim nation remains incomparable. No one loves his religion more than the Muslim loves Islam. Our faith becomes stronger with each challenge it faces and makes us more powerful.'[26]

## Rumours and riots

One knows that the time of violence is at hand from the content of rumours that now begin to circulate in the two communities.[27] Let us look more closely at some of the rumours that were circulating during one of the most horrendous episodes of communal violence in recent Indian history, the Gujarat riots of 2002.

On 27 February 2002, the Sabarmati Express was attacked, allegedly by a Muslim mob, at the railway station of Godhra, a small town near Ahmedabad in the state of Gujarat.[28] The train was carrying activists of the VHP, the religious arm of a resurgent Hindu nationalism, on their way back from Ayodhya, the legendary birthplace of Lord Rama, where the VHP was planning to construct a highly contentious temple—at the very site where the Babri mosque stood before it was demolished by a mob of Hindu nationalists.

In the attack on the train, around sixty Hindus, mostly men but also some women and children, were burnt alive when their coach was set on fire, it is commonly believed, by the mob (the cause of the fire has not been conclusively established). Two days after the gory incident, riots broke out in many parts of Gujarat, especially in the central districts of the state where both Godhra and Ahmedabad are located. The violence lasted for over a month and claimed more than a thousand lives, a vast majority of them Muslim.

The city of Ahmedabad, with a population of more than five million, the commercial, cultural and political capital of Gujarat (Gandhinagar, the actual state capital, is more or less a suburb of Ahmedabad), was the worst affected by the riots. Ahmedabad has a tradition of Hindu–Muslim violence going back more than thirty years. Indeed, isolated incidents of violence continued to be reported more than six months after the high tide of murder, arson and looting had subsided.

A Hindu informant remembered the reception of rumours thus: 'Every day, night or day, many rumours reached us. They tormented all of us. People couldn't sleep at night. For three months, the rumours deprived us of sleep. They had a very strong effect on women and children; women used to weep after hearing a new rumour and couldn't carry out their household tasks. Men used to stand at crossroads, meet people from outside their locality and ask about what was happening in other areas. They would then tell others.'

Deriving from the paranoid potential which lies buried in

all of us, rumours are the conversational food that helps in the growth of a collective 'community body'. There is little doubt that rumours are the fuel and riots the fire in which a heightened sense of community is also forged. Lending words and images, however horrific, to the imminent threat of deathly violence against the self and one's community, rumours give rise to complex emotions, not only the feelings of dread and danger but also of exhilaration at the transcendence of individual boundaries and the feelings of closeness and belonging to an entity beyond one's self.

Almost half of the rumours in Ahmedabad were common to both Hindus and Muslims: 'Don't buy anything from the bakery; it will be poisoned'; 'The milk has been poisoned. Poison has been injected into the milk pouches'. Except for changes in technology—milk in pouches instead of being delivered by vendors; bakeries instead of grocery shops—some of these rumours seem to be perennial since they have circulated in most riots over the last six decades. During the riots in Rohtak following Partition, there were rumours among the Hindus that milk vendors had been bribed by the Muslims to poison the milk.[29] Four children were said to be lying unconscious and two dogs had died (in Ahmedabad in 2002, it was a cat) after having drunk the poisoned milk; many claimed to have personally seen the dogs in the throes of death. Women had hurried to empty out the pails of milk, and they said strange sticky patches of white soon covered the cobbled stones of the streets. It was reported that Muslims had broken into grocery shops in the night and mixed powdered glass with the salt. A police van was said to be driving around the town, warning people not to buy salt.

We would call these perennial rumours about poisoned food—food that kills instead of nourishing—fundamental rumours. Fundamental in the sense that they attack what the psychoanalyst Erik Erikson called our sense of 'basic trust', received in our earliest experiences with an empathic mother, that lets us experience 'inside' and 'outside' as an interrelated goodness.[30] Poisoned milk makes the secure maternal presence we carry inside us recede. It breaches the individual's 'background of safety', releasing our paranoid potential and its accompanying persecutory anxiety.[31] The persecution anxiety is further heightened by another rumour common to both groups which attributes danger to hitherto safe activity in common public spaces, such as travel by train and bus.

The second category of rumours that can also be described as perennial has to do with sexual violence. In our particular case, this category is represented in both communities by rumours about the rape of the community's women and, additionally, among Hindus, by the threat of castration of its men: 'Don't let girls go out of the house. They kidnap them and do 'bad things' with them'; 'They are saying they will castrate all the infidels so that the whole race dies out.'

In undermining our familiar controls over mental life, a riot is like a midwife for unfamiliar, disturbing fantasies and complex emotions. The overcharged atmosphere of violence breathed day in and day out by a person lifts the lid on the cauldron of instinctual drives as civilized sensibility threatens to collapse. Rumours of sexual violence during a riot, and the mixture of horror and relish with which they are recounted, also release the more shameful excitement that bespeaks instinctual desire in its rawer form. Besides expressing moral outrage, rape rumours may also be used by the men as an unwanted but wished for vicarious satisfaction of their sadistic impulses. Perfectly ordinary men talk at length about rape and defilement in graphic language otherwise encountered only in extreme, psychopathic pornography.

Besides the commonality of some rumours to both communities, there are others that are group specific and betray the distinct and long-standing fears of each community that rise up to the surface during a riot.

In the case of Muslims, these rumours relate to a perceived threat to their religious identity: 'Islam is in danger', 'They are breaking our mosques', 'Now they will try to convert us to Hinduism, be vigilant', 'They force Muslims to say the name of Rama and kill you if you refuse.' These rumours are born of a religious minority's fear of being drowned in the sea of the majority. Thus, to protect themselves from possession by malignant spirits, of which minor Hindu divinities—the *devi*s and *devata*s—are considered the most dangerous, Muslims all over the subcontinent are enjoined to be pious and constantly proclaim their faith. Such calls to the battle stations of faith reflect the primary fear of Indian Muslims of somehow lapsing from the faith and becoming reabsorbed by the insidious Hindu society that surrounds them.

Other rumours, specific to the Muslim community although not among the most frequently mentioned, relate to the role of the police. 'Muslims are being arrested and taken away by the police' or 'The police are beating any Muslim found on the streets' or 'The police are taking away Muslims in trucks and dumping them in Hindu areas where they are killed' are some of the rumours that are a reflection on the partisan role of the predominantly Hindu police. Indeed, in many towns and cities of North India, such as Meerut, confrontations between the police and the Muslims have led to violent explosions.

The community-specific Hindu fear is encapsulated by rumours such as 'Large amounts of arms and ammunition have been sent to the Muslims from Pakistan' and 'Terrorists have infiltrated from across the Kachch border and spread all over Gujarat.' The mention of 'terrorists' makes these rumours the contemporary version of the rumour heard during the 1969 Ahmedabad riot of armed Pakistani agents seen parachuting into the city at night.

Here, by linking it with an armed and dangerous enemy, the Muslim minority becomes a psychological threat that is otherwise not justified by its numbers. The rumours reflect and revive the Hindu nationalist's deep-seated distrust of Muslim loyalty to the Indian state and a doubt regarding Muslim patriotism if the community is faced with a choice between the country of its birth and that of its coreligionists across the border. The rumours conjure up images of a vast Islamic army poised at the country's borders, of medieval Muslim marauders like Mahmud, the sultan of the kingdom of Ghazni, one of the most cruel and rapacious of Muslim invaders, who swept over North India every year like a monsoon of fire and was famed far and wide as the scourge of the Hindus.

Are the rumours during a religious riot also gendered, in the sense that some are more frequently to be found in the discourse of women than of men? They are not gendered as far as the most common rumours are concerned. However, women, both Hindu and Muslim, seem to show a preference for the more apocalyptic ones. 'Now there will be war and India will be destroyed', 'They are saying, "Hindus have darkened the sky [with arson], Muslims will dye the earth red [with Hindu blood]', 'Bhagwan has taken birth; not a single Muslim will survive now'—these are only three such rumours favoured by Hindu women. 'It is coming to pass as written down in the Quran: universal destruction' is their counterpart among Muslim women. Women, not unexpectedly, are also partial to rumours pertaining to the safety of their children, in the sense that more rumours about the kidnapping of children by the enemy community circulate among women than among men.

Rumours, then, are the motors of violence when individuals begin to feel helpless and frightened (but also manically exhilarated), loosened from their traditional cognitive moorings and thus prepared to give up previously held social, economic or political explanations for communal conflict. The strong anxiety accompanying the birth of violence can take many people away from 'knowing' and back to the realm of 'unknowing'—from a 'knowledge' of the cause of their distress to a state where they do not know what it is that makes them anxious though they *do* know that they are in distress. One antidote to paralysing anxiety is anger, preferably in a violent assertion that is psychically mobilizing, a violence almost invariably viewed by its perpetrators as pre-empting the enemy's imminent attack.[32]

Amplified by rumours, stoked by religious demagogues, the persecutory anxiety signals the imminent annihilation of one's group identity and must be combated by its forceful assertion. Acting demonstratively in terms of this identity as a Hindu or Muslim, though, threatens members of the rival community who too mobilize their religious identity as a defence. The spiral of religious rhetoric on one side triggering the same on the other, of threats and reactive counter-threats further fuels persecutory anxiety, and only the slightest spark is now needed for a violent explosion.

The involvement of religious rather than other social identities does not dampen but, on the contrary, increases the violence of the conflict. Religion brings to conflict between groups a greater emotional intensity and a deeper motivational thrust than language, region or other markers of ethnic identity. This is at least true of countries where the salience of religion in collective life is very high, as it is in India. With its historical allusions from sacred rather than profane history, its metaphors and analogies having their source in sacred legends, the religious justification of conflict involves fundamental values and releases some of our most violent passions. Moreover, rhythms of religious ritual, whether in common prayer, processions or other congregational activities, are particularly conducive to breaking down boundaries between the individual members of a group and thus, in times of tension and threat, forging violent mobs.

As for the actual violence, most people do not take part in

the looting, arson and the killings. These acts are generally the province of certain young men and older veterans of the community's violence although everyone—man, woman, child—will pitch in when their own house or neighbourhood is being attacked by a mob. The *goonda*s, the experts in violence, play a leading role; not only because of their expertise but also because of the moral 'high' the riot affords them. For the duration of the riot, they are no longer despised but see themselves, and are seen by their community, as soldiers protecting the community and its faith.

As for the role of politicians, there is little doubt of their involvement although their influence on the course taken by a riot is often exaggerated. Eyeing electoral gain, politicians certainly use the riot after the fact and may try to organize it in advance but usually find that the rioting mobs will not act according to their plans.

## Moralities of violence

The large-scale replacement of personal identities by a communal identity in a riot does not mean that people are now in some regressed, amoral primitive state where the violent side of human nature is bound to be unleashed randomly. The replacement of personal by communal identity only means a refocusing, and the individual now acts according to the norms of the communal Hindu or Muslim group. For instance, in a riot, there is a very different code of morality—not its absence—that governs the actions of both Hindus and Muslims. In both groups, arson, looting and killing men of the other community are no longer the serious transgressions they would be in times of peace. Yet, among both Hindus and Muslims, there is a consensual condemnation of rape and killing of the women of the other community. In Hyderabad, where riots have been frequent, the two communities share in common the commandments 'Thou shall not kill a woman' and 'Thou shalt not rape', although the intensity of outrage associated with the transgression of these commandments varies with and within the communities. Both communities view a riot as a battle exclusively between men in defence of the honour of their 'nations'. Women, for the most part, are noncombatants in this war.

In Hyderabad, the tradition of violence between the religious communities, the almost annual bloodletting, has developed certain norms which strongly disapprove of rape as a vehicle of contempt, rage or hatred that one community may feel for the other. Moreover, unlike some other ethnic/religious conflicts, such as the one in Bosnia, Hindus and Muslims still have to live together after a riot, carry out a minimal social and considerable economic interaction. Rape makes such interactions impossible and turns Hindu–Muslim animosity into implacable hatred. Like nothing else, it draws impermeable boundaries between the groups, separates them in an enmity where there is no longer a bridge between the two.

Not that there are no incidents of sexual violence. Accounts of such incidents, though, are almost always highly exaggerated. They seem to be necessary heralds of violence, events without which the tale of violence between the two communities will be only half-told, the account incomplete.

At an emotionally more neutral level, Hindus and Muslims also share a common disapproval of acts which hurt the religious sentiments of the other community. Such acts as throwing the carcass of a pig in a mosque or that of a cow in a Hindu temple, archetypal precipitating incidents for a riot— in the sense that there is an unarticulated expectation that such an incident should belong to the beginning of an account of a Hindu–Muslim riot—draw condemnation even at times when communal identities are rampant. This disapproval is often couched in terms of empathy: 'Their religious feelings are the

same as ours and we would not like it if it were done to us.'
The existence of this empathy, even in a time of murderous
violence, prevents a complete dehumaniztion of the 'enemy',
from a Hindu or Muslim considering the other as subhuman.

## The future of Hindu–Muslim conflict

The awareness of belonging to either one religious community
or the other—being Hindu or Muslim—has increased manifold
in recent years.

Every time violence between religious groups occurs in
India or in some other part of the subcontinent, the reach and
spread of modern communications ensure that a vast number
of people are soon aware of the incident. Each riot and its
aftermath raise afresh the issue of an individual's identification
with his religious group and bring it up to the surface of every
individual's consciousness in one way or another. This
awareness may be fleeting for some, last over a period of time
for others, but the process is almost always through a pre-
conscious self-interrogation on the significance of the religious
community for one's sense of identity. For varying periods of
time, individuals consciously experience their identity through
their religious group rather than through groups based on
caste, language, region or occupation. The duration of this
period, or even whether there will be a permanent change in
the mode of identity experience for some who will henceforth
encase themselves in the armour of an aggressive communal
identity, depends on many factors. Not least is the success of
revivalist and fundamentalist political outfits in encouraging
such a change.

As for the future, there is more than one scenario for the
likely evolution of Hindu–Muslim relations. The Hindu
nationalist, who views the conflict as a product of Hindu and
Muslim religious-cultural traditions, believes the only way of

avoiding large-scale violence is a change in the Muslim view of the community's role, traditions and institutions so that the Muslim can 'adapt' to the Hindu majority's culture. To ask the Muslims to recognize themselves in the Hindu nationalist version of Indian history, to expect them to feel their culture confirmed in Hindu symbols, rituals and celebrations is asking them to renounce their religious-cultural identity and to erase their collective memory so that they become indistinguishable from their Hindu neighbours. To be swamped by the surrounding Hindu culture has been the greatest fear of the Indian Muslim, articulated even by some medieval Sufis who are commonly regarded as closest to the Hindu tradition and as exemplars of the 'composite, syncretic tradition'. Such an assimilation is feared precisely *because* it is so tempting, holding the promise of a freedom from the fear of violence and an active and full participation in the majority culture. The Hindu nationalist's dilemma is that the Muslims continue to decline an offer that he believes is one that they cannot refuse. And so the nationalist finds that the Muslim is too big to either swallow or spit out.

The secularist, who views the conflict as rooted in socio-economic considerations, is more sanguine on the future of Hindu–Muslim relations. The secularist believes that in the long run the economic development of India will alter the socio-structural conditions and thus consign the conflict, as the cliché would have it, 'to the dust heap of history' as religious identities fade away and play less and less of a role in private and, especially, in public life. However, we need to sound a sceptical note on the belief in the primacy of political and economic structures in the shaping of consciousness. Cultural traditions—including the beliefs regarding the devilish 'Other'—are transmitted through the family and have a line of development separate from the political and economic systems of a society. What we would like to believe (that is, hope) is that we are moving towards an era of recognizing Hindu–Muslim differences rather than pursuing their chimerical commonalities. That we are moving towards a multicultural society rather than a 'composite' culture. Such multiculturalism is neither harmful nor dangerous but necessary since it enables different religious groups to deal with the modernizing process in an active way rather than withdraw in lamentation at the inequities of modernization or endure it as passive victims. We may have to give up Gandhi's dream of 'lasting heart unity' and content ourselves with the creation of a common public realm while regarding the other community with 'benign indifference' in private. There will be inevitable violence on the way. In the long run one can only hope that there will be a declining acceptance of religious hatred and a general disapproval of violence in the service of faith. In the short term, there is no alternative to what the political scientist Donald Horowitz claims is vital for the prevention of ethnic riots all over the world, namely the effective deployment of force by the state, especially in the period of lull, that is, the twelve to twenty-four hours between the first incident and the major outbreak of violence.[33] Where the required political will is weak or absent, as appeared to be the case in Gujarat in 2002, the horrors of mass violence soon overcome any well-meaning effort at containing riots.

# THE INDIAN MIND

*I*n this book we have attempted to describe the manifestations of the spirit of India in various facets of Indian life and thought. By 'the spirit of India' we do not mean something elusive and ethereal, but are talking of the culturally shared part of the mind, a certain Indian-ness, that is reflected in the way the inhabitants of the subcontinent approach the daily tasks as well as the eternal questions of human existence. What are the building blocks of this Indian-ness which we have encountered in the foregoing chapters? Let us begin with the Indian (here, again, primarily the Hindu) view of the world.

## THE HINDU WORLD VIEW

Every civilization has a unique way of looking at the world. This world view, the civilization's centre of gravity, is a cluster of ideas which define the goal of human existence, the ways to reach this goal, the errors to be avoided and the obstacles to be expected on the way. The world view interprets central human experiences and answers perennial questions on what is good and what is evil, what is real and what is unreal, what is the essential nature of men and women and the world they live in, and what is man's connection to nature, to other human beings and to the cosmos.

For instance, if we look at China (and Chinese societies around the world), we can define the following elements in the dominant, Confucian world view: There is no other world than the one we live in. The ultimate meaning of life is embedded in and not separate from ordinary practical living. The meaning of life is then realized through a personal self-cultivation within the community and through mutual aid in the family, clan, school and workplace. The glue that binds society is not law but what the Chinese call *li*, a civilized mode of conduct. A predominant feature of the Chinese world view is a sense of duty rather than the demand for rights.

Similarly, in India, there are identifiable, specific elements in the dominant, Hindu world view. Here, we are not concerned so much with philosophical doctrines that are relevant only for religious and intellectual elites, but with the beliefs and attitudes—many of them not conscious—of a vast number of Indians that are reflected in their lives, their songs and their stories. These beliefs are disseminated through myths and legends, proverbs and metaphors, enacted in religious rituals, conveyed through tales told to children, given a modern veneer in Bollywood films and television serials, and glimpsed in the admonitions of parents or in the vision they have of their children's future. The world view that we are talking about, then, is absorbed from early on in life, and not through the head but the heart.

Three interlinked elements comprise a major part of the Hindu world view: moksha, dharma and karma. Our interest in these concepts is not philosophical, textual or historical, but psychological. What we want to look at closely is the contribution of this ancient trinity in the formation of the Indian mind and its reverberations in the thoughts and actions of contemporary Indians.[1]

## Moksha, the goal of life

Moksha, which variously means self-realization, transcendence, salvation, a release from this world, has been traditionally viewed by the Hindus as the goal of human life. The idea of moksha is intimately linked with the Indian conviction in the existence of another, 'higher' level of reality beyond the shared, verifiable, empirical reality of our world, our bodies and our emotions. A fundamental value of most schools of Hinduism (and the Sufis of Islam) is the belief in the existence of an 'ultimate' reality—related to everyday reality in the same way that waking consciousness is related to a dream—and it is an unquestioned verity of Indian culture, the common thread in the teachings of the culture's innumerable gurus. This 'ultimate' reality, whose apprehension is considered to be the highest goal and meaning of human life, is said to be beyond conceptual thought and indeed beyond mind. Intellectual thought, naturalistic science and other passions of the mind seeking to grasp the empirical nature of our world thus have a relatively lower status in the culture as compared to meditative practices or even art, since aesthetic and spiritual experiences are supposed to be closely related. In the culture's belief system, the aesthetic power of music and verse, of a well-told tale and a well-enacted play make them more, rather than less, real than life.

This emphasis on the spiritual which underlies the practices of the various schools of 'self-realization', such as those of Yoga, colours the emotional tone of the way an Indian looks at life. To most Indians, life is a combination of the tragic and the romantic. It is tragic in so far as they see human experience pervaded by ambiguities and uncertainties where man has little choice but to bear the burden of unanswerable questions, inescapable conflicts and incomprehensible afflictions of fate. But superimposed on the tragic, the Indian vision of moksha offers a romantic quest. The new journey is a search, and the seeker, if he withstands the perils of the road, will be rewarded by exaltation beyond normal human experience.

The belief in the existence of an 'ultimate reality', this nostalgia of the Indian soul, is a beacon of 'higher feeling' in the lives of most Indians, cutting across class and caste distinctions, bridging the distance between rural and urban, between the illiterate and the educated, between the rich and the poor. The ironic vision of life, which brings a detached and self-deprecating perspective on the tragic and in which gods have feet of clay, is rarely found among Indians. Even among those living in enclaves of Western modernity, an ironic stance towards the spiritual is at the most an affectation of a few young people which normally disappears as they begin to age.

If spirituality has been at the centre of the Indian world image, it would be reasonable to expect that it has continued to condition the Indian mind, colouring its intellectual, artistic and emotional responses in certain distinctive ways. In other words, there are various cultural consequences of this belief. One of these is the pervasive presence of hope, even in the most dismal of life circumstances. For centuries, Indian civilization has conveyed to the growing child the almost somatic conviction that there is an order, even if hidden and unknown, to our visible world. That there is a design to life that can be trusted in spite of life's sorrows, cruelties and injustices. The Indian mind, then, tends to convert even the slightest ray of hope into a blaze of light. Consider this man from a village in Rajasthan who is living in a Delhi slum. He works a back-breaking fourteen hours a day on a construction site, lives with six other members of his family in a single-room tenement and eats, if at all, stale food in a chipped enamel plate. Yet he rejects the idea of life being better in his village with surprised astonishment. The city, with its possibilities, for example schooling for his children, has provided him with a sliver of hope. The cynic might see his aspirations for a better life as completely unrealistic, look at him as someone who clutches at the thinnest of straws, who has never learnt that there is something as hoping too much, or hoping in vain. But what keeps this man and so many millions of others cheerful and expectant even under the most adverse economic, social and political circumstances is precisely this hope which is a sense of possession of the future, however distant that future may be.

Another consequence of the spiritual orientation, the unshakeable belief in a 'higher' reality, is the average Indian's fascination with and respect for the occult and its practitioners. Astrologers, soothsayers, clairvoyants, fakirs and other shamanic individuals who abound in Indian society are profoundly esteemed for they are thought to be in some kind of contact with the ultimate reality. In India, it is the 'god-men', the gurus, rather than political, social or intellectual leaders, who have come to incorporate our childhood yearning for omniscience and perfection in parental figures. Scholars or the scientists may be respected, but only the 'holy men', the men of god, are revered. Their presumed contact with another reality is supposed to confer on them supernatural powers, superhuman status and a moral excellence that is beyond the ordinary lot.

Psychologically, perhaps the most important consequence of the Hindu spiritual orientation, the widespread belief in the ultimate reality, the divinity immanent within each human being, is the feeling of self-worth that comes from a pre-conscious conviction of one's metaphysical significance. However socially demeaned or economically irrelevant a person may be in day-to-day life, the feeling of being central to the universe and not banished to its remote extremities, of being connected equally with everyone else to the *Urgrund* of human existence, quietly nourishes the individual's self-esteem and stands as a bulwark against despair and rage at life's inequities.

## Right and wrong

If moksha is the goal of life, then dharma, variously translated as law, moral duty, right action, conformity with the truth of things, is the means through which man approaches the desired goal. Today, there is widespread bemoaning of the lack of dharma in social institutions and individual lives. Traditional and modern Indians agree that there is hardly any institution left where those in positions of power have not veered away from dharma. Whereas modern Indians will also point to the great social churning that is taking place with the advent of modern egalitarian ideologies, traditionalists see the disappearance of dharma as solely responsible for the social conflict, oppression and unrest that characterize contemporary Indian society. And as for dharma in individual lives, here too the oft-heard lament is that things are not as they were. At one time, in the utopian long, long ago, every person knew that it was not what he did that was important for his spiritual progress but whether he acted in conformity with his dharma. The activity itself—whether that of a shoemaker or a priest, a housewife or a farmer, a social worker serving others and alleviating misery or an ascetic apparently indifferent to the suffering around him—was considered equally good and equally right if it was consistent with dharma. And since traditional Indians are inclined to tell stories whenever they wish to prove a point or convey what the world is like or ought to be like, using narrative as a way of thinking and as an inquiry into the nature of reality, they are likely to tell a story very much like this one:

> There was once a king who was strolling along the banks of the Ganga with an entourage of his ministers. It was the monsoon season and the river was in spate, its swirling waters rushing towards the sea. The broad sweep of the swollen river and its strong current filled the king with awe. Suddenly mindful of his own insignificance, he addressed his

ministers: 'Is there no one on this earth who can reverse the flow of this river so that it flows from the sea to the mountains?' The ministers, shaking their heads, smiled at the king's naivety. But a prostitute who overheard his question stepped forward and addressed the river thus: 'O Mother Ganga, if I have striven to fulfil my dharma as a whore by giving my body to all comers, without distinguishing rich from poor, handsome from ugly, old from young, then reverse your flow!' The waters stood still for a moment, as if in deliberation, and then the river started flowing backwards.

Today, the conservatives will continue, the ideologies of Western modernity with their notions of egalitarianism and individual choice, their highlighting the importance of material rewards rather than the spirit of human activity, their emphasis on human aspirations rather than limits, have led to widespread social envy, unbridled greed and selfishness in Indian society. Most would achingly agree that of the major elements of the traditional Hindu world view, dharma is the one that is most endangered and perhaps already crumbling under the impact of modernity. Yet there is one aspect of dharma that continues to be of vital importance in understanding the Indian mind, and not only that of the orthodox Hindu. For even if one rejects many traditional values associated with dharma, it is still pivotal in the formation of the Indian ethical sensibility.

The main feature of this sensibility, in which it diverges from its Islamic and Judeo-Christian counterparts, is a pronounced ethical relativism which has become entrenched in the Hindu way of thinking. For how does any individual *know* what is right action, that he is acting in accordance with moral law and in 'conformity with the truth of things'? The traditional answer has been that he cannot since right action depends on the culture of his country (*desa*), the historical era in which he lives (*kala*), on the efforts required of him at his particular stage of life (*srama*) and, lastly, on the innate character (*guna*) that he has inherited from a previous life. An individual can never know the configuration of all these factors in an absolute sense, nor even significantly influence them. Nor is there a book, or its authoritative interpreters such as the Church, which can help by removing doubts on how the individual must act in each conceivable situation. 'Right' and 'wrong', then, are relative; depending on its specific context, every action can be right—or wrong.

In lessening the burden of the individual's responsibility for his actions, the cultural view of right action alleviates the guilt suffered in some societies by those whose actions transgress rigid thou-shalt and thou-shalt-not axioms. Instead, an Indian's actions are governed by a more permissive and gentle, but more ambiguous, thou-canst-but-try ethos. On the one hand, this basic uncertainty makes possible the taking of unconventional and risky actions; on the other hand, actions are accompanied by a pervasive doubt as to the wisdom of individual initiative, making independent voluntary action rare for many who look for psychological security by acting as one's ancestors did in the past and as one's social group— primarily the caste—does at present. The relativism of dharma supports tradition *and* modernity, innovation and conformity.

The ethical relativism of dharma has been broadened by the late poet-scholar A.K. Ramanujan to embrace the very way Indians think in most situations. In his stimulating essay 'Is There an Indian Way of Thinking?'[2] Ramanujan begins his exposition with a survey of Indian intellectuals done some thirty years ago where they were asked to describe the 'Indian Character'. As one can imagine, given the Indian talent for self-criticism, the intellectuals wrote quite sharp comments. They all seemed to agree on one thing: the Indian trait of hypocrisy. Indians don't mean what they say, and say different things at different times. Many occidental travellers in the last centuries complain about the same thing and, in fact, in the famed Indologist Max Mueller's lectures of 1883 on India, he felt compelled to counter these accusations by writing a chapter called 'Truthful Character of Indians'.[3]

The Indian inconsistency is still regarded as puzzling: How can a reputed astronomer, working at a well-known institute of fundamental sciences, also be a practicing astrologer? How can the Western-educated executive of a multinational corporation consult horoscopes and holy men for family decisions? Why does an Oxford-educated cabinet minister postpone an important meeting because the hour is astrologically inauspicious for a meeting?

These observed traits of inconsistency, however, Ramanujan asserts, have nothing to do with the level of a person's education or logical rigour. They are better understood if we recognize that different cultures seem to prefer either context-free or context-sensitive rules in their thought processes and that Indians operate on the basis of context-sensitivity rather than context-freedom. Let us elaborate.

There is no notion of a *universal* human nature in Indian culture and thus we cannot deduce ethical rules like 'Man shall not kill' or 'Man shall not tell an untruth' or any other unitary law for all men. What a person should or should not do depends on the context. Thus Manu, the ancient Indian law giver, has the following to say: 'A kshatriya [a man belonging to the warrior castes], having defamed a brahmin, shall be fined one hundred [*panas*]; a vaishya [someone belonging to the farmer and merchant castes] one hundred and fifty or two hundred; a shudra [a man belonging to the servant castes] shall suffer corporal punishment.'[4] Even truth-telling is not an unconditional imperative. Here is a quotation from another law book: 'An untruth spoken by people under the influence of anger, excessive joy, fear, pain or grief, by infants, by very old men, by persons labouring under a delusion or being under the influence of drink, does not cause the speaker to fall [that is, it is not a sin].'[5]

The Christian injunction against coveting 'thy neighbour's wife' is shared by Hindu law books, which proclaim that 'in this world there is nothing as detrimental to long life as criminal conversation with another man's wife.' In fact, Hindus are even stricter in defining adultery; talking to a woman alone in the forest, 'or at the confluence of rivers', offering her presents, touching her ornaments and dress, sitting with her on a bed, are all adulterous acts. The nature of punishment, of course, depends on the respective castes of the adulterous couple and there are also exceptions, such as the one which condones adultery with 'the wives of actors and singers'.[6] Though it contains a chapter with the title 'Other Men's Wives', the *Kamasutra*, too, shares the Hindu disapproval of adultery. But here again there are exceptions to the rule, for instance, if your unrequited passion makes you fall sick, and once these have been listed, Vatsyayana proceeds to outline the various ways to seduce other men's wives.[7] His position seems to be: You shouldn't do it. But if you must, then these are the ways to proceed. But, of course, you shouldn't have done it in the first place.

Virtues, too, are as dependent on the context as are transgressions. Bravery may be a virtue for the kshatriya, the warrior, but it is certainly not one for the baniya, the merchant. Ramanujan remarks that for a Western-Christian tradition, which is based on the premise of universalization—the golden rule of the New Testament—such a view that each class of men has its own laws, its own proper ethics, which cannot be universalized must be baffling and, ultimately, a producer of denigration.

Context-sensitivity is not just a feature of traditional moral law but extends to many areas of contemporary Indian life and thought. The cultural psychologist Richard Shweder, who has compared descriptive phrases used by Oriyas from eastern India and mid-westerners from the United States, has shown that the two describe persons very differently.[8] Americans characterize a person with abstract, generic words like 'good', 'nice', while the Oriyas use more concrete, contextual descriptions like 'he helps me', 'brings sweets', etc. The descriptions provided by the Indians were more situation-specific and more relational than those of Americans. Indian descriptions focus on behaviour. They describe what was done, where it was done, and to whom or with whom it was done. The Indian respondents said, 'He has no land to cultivate but likes to cultivate the land of others,' or 'When a quarrel arises, he cannot resist the temptation of saying a word,' or 'He behaves properly with guests but feels sorry if money is spent on them.' It is the behaviour itself that is focal and significant rather than the inner attribute that supposedly underlies it. This tendency to supply the context when providing a description characterizes the descriptions of Indians regardless of social class, education or level of literacy. It appears, then, that the preferred Indian way of describing people is not due to a lack of skill in abstracting concrete instances to form a general proposition, but rather a consequence of the fact that global inferences about people are typically regarded as neither meaningful nor informative.

If truth is relative, something you are never destined to know, then there is no choice but to be tolerant of the truth of others. The story of the six blind men who argued over the nature of an elephant, based on which part of the beast each man had explored with his hands, is a cautionary tale that could only be Hindu in its inspiration. The roots of the vaunted Hindu tolerance, then, may well lie in this context-dependent way of thinking. Yet because of its intimate connection with matters of religious faith, to a person's deepest values, this particular civilizational heritage of ethical action being inseparable from its context does show some variation across religious communities.

We see this when we look at the moral judgements of Hindus and Muslims on their interactions with each other, both in times of peace and conflict.[9] There are many such interactions in normal times: eating with a member of the opposite community, working with him, punishing a member of the other community who is making fun of your religious symbols or insulting a woman of your community. And then there are the interactions during a riot: killing, arson and rape. As compared to the Muslims, the Hindus were much more relativistic and contextual in judging a behaviour as a transgression and more easy-going in proposing punishment for actions judged as wrong. Irrespective of age and gender, 'It all depends' was an almost reflexive response. When it came to cases of interaction with the Muslims, the answers were almost always framed in terms of a context, temporal or spatial. The linkage of morality with time would be typically expressed thus: '[Killing] was wrong when times were different but it is not wrong now.' The individual can thus convincingly state that an action is wrong in right times but right in wrong times. Similarly, space is also involved in moral judgements. Hindus often said that actions such as beating up a Muslim or arson or looting of Muslim shops during a riot were wrong if you lived in a Muslim-majority area but all right if you were living in a Hindu-majority neighbourhood. As a result of this contextual stance, wrong actions by the members of one's own community evoked far less emotion and righteousness than the corresponding actions among the Muslims. In this particular instance Muslims were more definite and unambiguous about which actions were right and which were clearly wrong, even during a riot.

The moral relativism of the Hindu mind is not an *absence* of moral code but only a more context-sensitive way of looking at and dealing with its violation. In many ways, Hindus are extremely strict in their definition of what constitutes a deviation from morality. Consider a popular story from the *Mahabharata*, the epic whose centerpiece is the great war between the forces of good and evil, represented by the Pandavas and the Kauravas, respectively. (Of course, given the Hindu penchant for relativity, good and evil are not polar opposites: Yuddhishtira, the most virtuous of the Pandava brothers, who had never told an untruth in his life, was a compulsive gambler; the mighty Bhima could not control his temper; another brother had a roving eye for women.) At one point in the war the Pandava army was being decimated by Drona's arrows. Drona, the great archer and teacher of both the Pandava and Kaurava princes, was one of the several good men who were fighting on the side of evil in this war, on account of their dharma, their moral duty. The Pandava brothers rushed to Lord Krishna who had agreed to advise them, and asked how they could stop Drona before he destroyed them.

'There is only one way,' Lord Krishna said. 'Drona loves his son Ashwathama more than his life. If he hears that Ashwathama is no more, he will lay down his bow and die.'

'But why should he believe us?' the Pandavas asked.

'The only one he will believe is Yuddhishtira, for every one knows that Yuddhishtira never lies,' Lord Krishna suggested.

Yuddhishtira, however, refused. 'I can never tell an untruth, even if it means we will lose this war.'

The Pandava princes again sought Krishna's counsel.

'Well,' said Krishna, 'You have in your forces an elephant with the same name as Drona's son. If you kill the elephant, then Yuddhishtira just has to say "Ashwathama is dead" and it will not be a lie.'

Yuddhishtira, however, was stubborn, maintaining that he would be stating a fact, not the truth. After much persuasion and warnings that evil would triumph on earth if he did not help, Yuddhishtira agreed that he would shout out across enemy lines, 'Ashwathama is dead...' then add in a normal tone of voice, '...but the elephant.'

The elephant was duly killed. Yuddhishtira shouted out the news of Ashwathama's death; when he came to 'but the elephant', the Pandavas began beating the war drums, so that Drona only heard the first part of the sentence. The foremost of archers laid down his bow and died of grief.

Many years after the great war was over and all the protagonists were dead, their souls began the journey to the next world, dropping out one by one on the long way to heaven. Only Yuddhishtira and his dog could come right up to heaven's gates, even Lord Krishna having to spend a little time in the netherworld for his part in the deceit that led to Drona's death. At heaven's gates, Yuddhishtira was told that he would have to spend one day in hell before he could enter.

'But why?' the virtuous Yuddhishtira protested. 'I have never told a lie in my life.'

'Perhaps,' he was informed, 'but on one occasion you did not tell the truth *loudly* enough.'

It is noteworthy that the virtuous Yuddhishtira had to atone for an almost nonexistent lapse because his context was that of integrity, of the 'man who never lies', while Krishna, the Lord of the Universe and thus of its moral order, got away with a slap on the wrist—considering his role in the lie—since his context here was not that of god but of a political and strategic adviser, where deception is *de rigeur*.

## Karma, rebirth and the Indian mind

The third essential idea of the Hindu world view is karma. The popular understanding of karma is expressed by a villager thus: 'Even at the time of death man should wish to do good deeds and wish to be reborn in a place where he can do good deeds again. After many lives of good deeds [living in dharma]

a man will attain mukti (another word for moksha). If he does
evil deeds, his form changes till he falls lower, till he becomes
a *jar* [an inanimate thing].'[10] Other Hindus, when pressed for
their sense of karma, are likely to express the same twin
ideas—namely, the cycles of birth and death in which an
individual soul progresses (or regresses) through various levels
of existence; and the control of this movement by the karma
of the individual soul, the balance of 'right' and 'wrong'
actions that accompany the individual from one birth to
another.

Psychologically, what interests us most in the karma theory
is its idea of innate dispositions (*samskaras*), a heritage of
previous life, with which a newborn is believed to come into
the world and which imposes certain limits on the socialization
of the child. In other words, Indians do not consider infant
nature as a *tabula rasa* which is infinitely malleable and can be
moulded in any direction desired by the parents. With the
cultural belief in the notion of samskaras, there is little social
pressure to foster the belief that if only the caretakers were
good enough and constantly on their toes, the child would
fulfil all his potential. With the Indian emphasis on man's
inner limits, there is not that sense of urgency and the struggle
against the outside world that often seem to propel Western
lives. Let us tell another story.

On the bank of the Ganga, there once lived a holy man
called Yajnavalkya together with his wife. One day, as he was
meditating, he felt something small and soft fall into the nest
of his hands. He opened his eyes and saw that it was a small
female mouse which must have fallen down from the claws of
an eagle circling above. The holy man took pity on the mouse,
and using his occult powers, transformed it into a small girl
and took her home. The girl grew up as the daughter of the
house, and when she reached marriageable age, Yajnavalkya's
wife reproached him one day, saying, 'Don't you see your

daughter is mature now and needs a husband?' Yajnavalkya answered, 'You are right. I have decided that she should have the best possible husband in all the worlds.' He then called the sun-god and when he appeared Yajnavalkya said, 'I have chosen you as my son-in-law.' He then turned to the girl and asked her, 'Would you like the light of three worlds as your husband?' But she answered, 'Ah father, he is much too plump and red-faced. Find me another husband.' The holy man smiled and asked the sun whether he knew of anyone who was better than him. The sun answered, 'O, holy man! The cloud is even stronger than I am, for it can cover me.' Yajnavalkya called the god of clouds, but once again when he asked his daughter's consent she replied, 'Oh, father, he looks much too morose. Find me a better husband.' Yajnavalkya asked the cloud whether there was someone in the world better than he. The cloud answered, 'The mountain is certainly better, for it can stop me.' The holy man called the mountain god, but the moment he appeared the girl cried out, 'Oh, Father, he is too massive and clumsy! Find me a better husband.' Yajnavalkya's patience was nearly exhausted, but since he loved his daughter, he asked the mountain whether he knew of someone who was even better. The mountain answered, 'The mouse can bore as many holes in me as it wants to. Considering that, it must be stronger than I am.' Yajnavalkya called the mouse, and as soon as the girl saw him, she exclaimed, 'Father! This is the only husband I can be happy with. Ah, can't you change me into a mouse?' The holy man fulfilled her wish. And as the two mice disappeared into the bushes, he walked back home, smiling to himself and saying, 'Although the sun, the cloud and the mountain stood before her as suitors, the mouse-girl needed to become a mouse again. Her innate nature could not be denied.'

The karmic balance from a previous life and thus the innate dispositions with which one enters the present one serve to make a Hindu more accepting of the inevitable disappointments that afflict even the most fortunate of lives. Yet whereas the notion of inherited dispositions can console and help to heal, it can also serve the purpose of denial of individual responsibility. Thus a thirty-year-old woman patient in psychotherapy, becoming aware of her aggressive impulses towards her husband as revealed in a dream, spontaneously exclaimed, 'Ah, these are due to my bad samskaras. However hard I try to be a good wife, my bad samskaras prevent me.'[11]

## I AND THE OTHER: SEPARATION AND CONNECTION

If each one of us begins life as a mystic, awash in a feeling of pervasive unity where there is no distance between ourselves and the outer world, then the process of sorting out a 'me' from 'not-me' is one of the primary tasks of our earliest years. The task involves the recognition, later taken for granted (at least in most of our waking hours and in a state of relative sanity), that I am separate from all that is not-I, that my 'Self' is not merged with but detached from the 'Other.' The experience of separation has its origins in our beginnings, although its echoes continue to haunt us till the end of life, agitating the mind, at times violently, in times of psychological or spiritual crisis.

The Indian gloss on the dilemmas and pain of banishment from the original feeling of oneness, the exile from the universe, has been to emphasize a person's enduring connection to nature, the Divine, and all living beings. This unitary vision, of *soma* and psyche, individual and community, self and world, is present in most forms of popular culture even today. From religious rites to folk festivals, from the pious devotion of communal singing in temples to the orgiastic excesses of holi, the festival of colours, there is a negation of separation and a celebration of connection.

The high cultural value placed on connection is, of course, most evident in the individual's relationships with others. The yearning for relationships, for the confirming presence of loved ones and the psychological oxygen they provide, is the dominant modality of social relations in India, especially within the extended family. Individuality and independence are not values that are cherished. It is not uncommon for family members who often accompany a patient for a first psychotherapeutic interview to complain about the patient's *autonomy* as one of the symptoms of his disorder. Thus the father and elder sister of a twenty-eight-year-old engineer who had a psychotic episode described their understanding of his chief problem as one of unnatural autonomy: 'He is very stubborn in pursuing what he wants, without taking our wishes into account. He thinks he knows what is best for him and does not listen to us. He thinks his own life and career are more important than the concerns of the rest of the family.'[12]

The high value placed on connection does not mean that an Indian is incapable of functioning when he is by himself or that he does not have a sense of his own agency. What it does imply is his greater need for ongoing mentorship, guidance and help from others in getting through life and a greater vulnerability to feelings of helplessness when these ties are strained.

The yearning for relationships, for the confirming presence of loved ones and the distress aroused by their unavailability in time of need, are more hidden in Western societies. There the dominant value system prizes autonomy, privacy and self-actualization, and holds that individual independence and initiative are 'better' than mutual dependence and community. But it depends, of course, on the culture's vision of a 'good society' and 'individual merit' whether a person's behaviour on the scale between fusion and isolation is nearer the pole of merger and fusion with others or the pole of complete isolation.

In other words, the universal polarities of individual versus relational, nearness versus distance in human relationships are prey to culturally fashioned beliefs and expectations. To borrow from Schopenhauer's imagery, human beings are like hedgehogs on a cold night. They approach each other for warmth, get pricked by the quills of the other and move away till, feeling cold, they again come closer. This to and fro movement keeps on being repeated till an optimum position is reached where the body temperature is above the freezing point yet the pain inflicted by the quills—the nearness of the other—is still bearable. The balancing point is different in various cultures. In India, as compared to modern European and North American cultures, the optimum position entails the acceptance of more pain in order to get greater warmth.

The emphasis on connection is also reflected in the Indian image of the body, a core element in the development of the mind. As we saw earlier, in the traditional medical system of Ayurveda, everything in the universe, animate or inanimate is believed to be made of five forms of matter. Living beings are only a certain kind of organization of matter. Their bodies constantly absorb the five elements of environmental matter. For Ayurveda, the human body is intimately connected with nature and the cosmos and there is nothing in nature without relevance for medicine. The Indian body image, then, stresses an unremitting interchange taking place with the environment, simultaneously accompanied by a ceaseless change within the body. Moreover, in the Indian view, there is no essential difference between body and mind. The body is merely the gross form of matter (*sthulasharira*), just as the mind is a more subtle form of the same matter (*sukshmasharira*); both are different forms of the same body–mind matter—*sharira*.

In contrast, the Western image is of a clearly etched body, sharply differentiated from the rest of the objects in the universe. This vision of the body as a safe stronghold with a limited number of drawbridges that maintain a tenuous contact with the outside world has its own cultural consequences. It seems to us that in Western discourse, both scientific and artistic, there is considerable preoccupation with what is going on *within* the fortress of the individual body. Pre-eminently, one seeks to explain behaviour through psychologies that derive from biology—to the relative exclusion of the natural and meta-natural environment. The contemporary search for a genetic basis to all psychological phenomena, irrespective of its scientific merit, is thus a natural consequence of the Western body image. The natural aspects of the environment—the quality of air, the quantity of sunlight, the presence of birds and animals, the plants and the trees—are a priori viewed, when they are considered at all, as irrelevant to intellectual and emotional development. Given the Western image of the body, it is understandable that the more 'far-out' Indian beliefs on the effects on the sharira of planetary constellations, cosmic energies, the earth's magnetic fields, seasonal and daily rhythms and precious stones and metals are summarily consigned to the realm of fantasy, where they are of interest solely to a 'lunatic fringe' of Western society.

It is not only the body but also the emotions that have come to be differently viewed because of the Indian emphasis on connection. As cultural psychologists have pointed out, such emotions as sympathy and feelings of interpersonal communion and shame that have to do with other persons become primary, while the more individualistic emotions such as anger and guilt are secondary. The Indian mind has a harder time experiencing and expressing anger and guilt but is more comfortable than the Western individualistic psyche in dealing with feelings of sympathy and shame. If pride is overtly expressed, it is often directed to a collective of whom the self is a part. Working very hard to win a promotion at work is only secondarily connected to the individual need for achievement, which is the primary driving motivation in the West. The first conscious or pre-conscious thought in the Indian mind is, 'How happy and proud my family will be!' This is why Indians tend to idealize their families and ancestral background, why there is such a prevalence of family myths and of family pride, and why the role models for the young are almost exclusively members of the family, very frequently a parent, rather than the movie stars, sporting heroes, or other public figures favoured by Western youth.

This greater 'dividual'[13] (in contrast to 'individual') or relational orientation is also congruent with the main thematic content of Indian art. In traditional Indian painting and, especially, in temple sculptures, man is not represented as a discrete presence but absorbed in his surroundings; the individual not separate but existing in all his myriad connections. These sculptures, as Thomas Mann observes in his Indian novella *The Transposed Heads*, are an 'all encompassing labyrinth flux of animal, human and divine...visions of life in the flesh, all jumbled together...suffering and enjoying in thousand shapes, teeming, devouring, turning into one another.'[14]

If one thinks of Eros not in its narrow meaning of sex but in its wider connotation of a loving 'connectedness' (where the sexual embrace is only the most intimate of all connections), then the relational cast to the Indian mind makes Indians more 'erotic' than many other peoples of the world. The relational orientation, however, also easily slips into conformity and conventional behaviour, making many Indians psychologically old even when young. On the other hand, the Western individualistic orientation has a tendency towards self-aggrandizement, 'the looking out for Number One', and the belief that the gratification of desires—most of them related to consumption—is the royal road to happiness. In a postmodern accentuation of 'fluid identities' and a transitional attitude toward relationships, of 'moving on', contemporary Western man (and the modern upper-class Indian) may well embody what the Jungians call *puer aeternus*—the eternal youth, ever in pursuit of *his* dreams, full of vitality, but nourishing only to himself while draining those around him.[15]

We are, of course, not advancing any simplified dichotomy between the Western cultural image of an individual, autonomous self and the relational, transpersonal self of Indian society. These are prototypical patterns that do not exist in their pure form in any society. Psychotherapy with patients of the Western middle-class tells us that autonomy of the self is as precarious in reality as is the notion of an Indian self that is merged in the surround of its family and community. Both visions of human experience are present in all the major cultures, though a particular culture may, over a length of time, highlight and emphasize one at the expense of the other. Historically, man's connection to the universe, especially his community, has also been an important value in Western tradition, though it may have been submerged at certain periods of history, especially in the nineteenth and early twentieth century. This, a so-called value of counter-enlightenment, is part of the relativist and sceptical tradition that goes back to Western antiquity. It stresses that belonging to a community is a fundamental need of man and asserts that only if a man truly belongs to such a community naturally and unselfconsciously can he enter the living stream and lead a full, creative and spontaneous life. Similarly, the celebration of the pleasures of individuality and of a desire-driven life, though muted, have not been completely absent in India and are indeed enjoying a resurgence among many modern Indians.

## MALE AND FEMALE

Another fundamental aspect of the Indian mind where it differs from its Western counterpart is related to the dawning realization in infancy of the difference between genders. It involves the acknowledgement and the profound realization for the child that all living beings and especially his beloved caretakers belong to either one sex or the other; they are either male or female.

This differentiation is of course universal but it is our cultural heritage that further elaborates what it means to be, look, think and behave like a man or a woman. This becomes clearer if one thinks of Greek or Roman sculpture which, we believe, has greatly influenced Western gender representations. Here, male gods are represented by hard muscled bodies and chests without any fat. One only needs to compare Greek and Roman statuary with the sculpted representations of Hindu gods, or the Buddha, where the bodies are softer, suppler and, in their hint of breasts, nearer to the female form. Many Buddhist images of Avalokiteswara ('the Lord who listens to the cries of the world') are of a slender boyish figure in the traditional feminine posture—weight resting on the left hip, right knee forward; they are the Indian precursor of the sexually ambiguous Chinese goddess Kuan Yin.[16] This minimizing of difference between male and female figures finds its culmination in the ardhanarishvara—'half-man and half-woman'—form of the great god Shiva who is portrayed with the secondary sexual characteristics of both sexes.

The visually lesser differentiation between male and female representations in Indian culture is further reinforced by its important, perhaps dominant, form of religiosity, which not only provides a sanction for man's feminine strivings, but raises these strivings to the level of a religious-spiritual quest. In devotional Vaishnavism, Lord Krishna alone is male and all devotees, irrespective of their sex, are female. It is a culture where one of the greatest Sanskrit poets of love, Amaru, a man, is believed to have been the hundred-and-first incarnation of a soul which had previously occupied the bodies of a hundred women; where the voice of the Tamil saint-poet Nammalavar—also a man—who wrote 370 poems on the theme of love, was always that of a woman.[17] It is a culture where in superior human beings feminine traits are joined to masculine ones. So a cultural hero like Gandhi can publicly proclaim that he had mentally become a woman, and that (well before the psychoanalyst Karen Horney) there is as much reason for a man to wish that he was born a woman as for women to do otherwise, and take it for granted that he will strike a responsive chord in his audience.

Given the variance in the cultural interpretations of the universal experience of gender differentiation, it is not surprising that the British in the colonial era labelled Indian men (excepting the 'warrior races' such as the Sikhs, Rajputs and Jats) as 'effeminate'. Such judgements are a reflexive outcome of deep-seated and rarely examined convictions on what is masculine and what feminine. Between a minimum of sexual differentiation that is required to function heterosexually with a modicum of pleasure, and a maximum which cuts off any sense of empathy and emotional contact with the other sex which is then experienced as a different species altogether, there is a whole range of positions, each occupied by a culture which insists on calling it the only one that is mature and healthy.

In conclusion, let us again emphasize that the Hindu world view, the relational orientation, the context-sensitivity and the lesser sexual differentiation that go into the formation of the Indian mind are not abstractions to be more or less hazily comprehended during the adult years. They are constituents of an Indian's psyche, absorbed by the child in his relationship with his caretakers from the very beginning of life as the underlying truth of the world. Rarely summoned for conscious examination, this cultural part of the mind is neither determinedly universal nor utterly idiosyncratic. The mental representation of our cultural heritage, it remains in constant conversation with the universal and individual aspects of our mind throughout life, each influencing and shaping the other two at every moment of our being.

# NOTES AND REFERENCES

## INTRODUCTION

1. G. Roth, Interview in *Die Zeit*, 23 February 2006, 36. (Our translation). For a good summary of the neurosciences view see, S. Pinker, *The Modern Denial of Human Nature* (London: Penguin Press Science, 2003).
2. J. McCrindle, *Ancient India as Described by Megasthenes and Arrian* (Calcutta: Chukkervertty, Chatterjee & Co.,1960), 100.
3. J.L. Nehru, *The Discovery of India* (Calcutta: Signet Press, 1946), 30.
4. N.C. Chaudhuri, *The Continent of Circe* (London: Chatto and Windus, 1965), 86.
5. The outer circle is becoming increasingly important with the progress of globalization. Thus, although there are books on the 'inner circle' in Europe, such as L. Barzini, *The Italians* (New York: Touchstone, 1996), G. Craig, *The Germans* (New York: Plume, 1991), K. Fox, *Watching the English* (London: Hodder & Stoughton, 2003), we predict that there will soon be a book on 'The Europeans' as Europe struggles to define a European identity in cultural-psychological terms as distinct from its political, geographical boundaries.

## THE HIERARCHICAL MAN

1. S.K. Datta-Ray, 'Where Rank Alone Matters', *The Times of India*, July 2005.

2. The various studies have been summarized by Patricia Uberoi in P. Uberoi, ed., *Family, Kinship and Marriage in India* (Delhi: Oxford University Press, 1993), 387.

3. In a recent survey of young people from the ages of 18 to 35 in 14 Indian cities (*India Today*, 26 February 2006, 44), 68 per cent of the respondents preferred to live in joint families, the percentage being slightly higher in males than females.

4. Much of the following is based on S. Kakar, *The Inner World: A Psychoanalytical Study of Childhood and Society in India* (Delhi and New York: Oxford University Press, 1978), chap. 3.

5. See also A. Béteille, 'The Family and the Reproduction of Inequality', in P. Uberoi, ed., *Family, Kinship and Marriage in India*, 435–51.

6. L. Dumont, *Homo Hierarchicus: The Caste System and its Implications*, tr. M. Sainsbury (Chicago: University of Chicago Press, 1970).

7. M. Lewis, *Language, Thought and Personality in Infancy and Childhood* (New York: Basic Books, 1964), 33.

8. S. Kakar, 'The Theme of Authority in Social Relations in India', *Journal of Social Psychology* 84, 1971, 93–101. The authority relations in the family are elaborated on in Kakar, *Inner World*, 119–20.

9. See also, J.S. Chhokar, 'Leadership and Culture in India', in J.S. Chhokar et al., eds., *Cultures, Leadership and Organizations: The GLOBE Book of Countries* (forthcoming); P. Singh & A. Bhandarker, *Corporate Success and Transformational Leadership* (New Delhi: Wiley Eastern, 1990).

10. J.B.P. Sinha, *The Nurturant Task Leader* (New Delhi: Concept, 1979).

11. S. Kakar et al., 'Leadership in Indian Organizations from a Comparative Perspective', *International Journal of Cross Cultural Management* 2:2, 2002, 239–50.

12. R.J. House et al., *Leadership, Culture and Organizations: The GLOBE Study of 62 Societies* (Thousand Oaks, California: Sage, 2004).

13. M. Javidan et al., 'Cross-Border Transfer of Knowledge: Cultural Lessons from Project GLOBE', *Academy of Management*

*Executive* 19:2, 2005, 59–76. The other comparisons are also taken from this article. For an earlier international study confirming the high power distance in Indian organizations see, G. Hofstede, *Culture's Consequences* (London: Sage, 1980).

14. Javidan, 63.
15. Older anthropological writings attest to this pattern being central to the father–son relationship; see, D.G. Mandelbaum, *Society in India* (Berkeley: University of California Press, 1970), vol.1, 60; A.C. Mayer, *Caste and Kinship in Central India* (London: Routledge, Kegan and Paul, 1970), 218; A.D. Ross, *The Hindu Family in its Urban Setting* (Toronto: University of Toronto Press, 1962), 10.
16. Kakar, *The Inner World*, 200–1.
17. Parmahansa Yogananda, *Autobiography of a Yogi* (Los Angeles: Self-Realization Fellowship, 1972), 268.
18. J.L. Roopnarine and P. Suppal, 'Kakar's Psychoanalytic Interpretation of Indian Childhood: The Need to Emphasize the Father and Multiple Caregivers in the Socialization Equation', in D. Sharma, ed., *Childhood, Family and Sociocultural Change in India* (Delhi: Oxford University Press, 2003), 115–37; see also S. Derne, 'Culture, Family Structure, and Psyche in Hindu India', in Sharma, 88–114.

## THE INNER EXPERIENCE OF CASTE

1. Dumont, *Homo Hierarchicus*, 43, calls it 'the opposition of pure and the impure'. Most leading authorities on the caste system have shared Dumont's view; see, for instance, F.G. Bailey, *Caste and the Economic Frontier* (Manchester: Manchester University Press, 1957); M. Mariott, 'Interactional and Attributional Theories of Caste Ranking', *Man* 39, 1959, 92–107; M.N. Srinivas, *Caste in Modern India and Other Essays* (Bombay: Asia Publishing House, 1962), 150–1. Although some writers on caste have proposed other ordering principles of caste hierarchy, for example, the opposition of auspicious and inauspicious (Raheja; Das and Uberoi), status difference (Milner; Sheth), most scholars subscribe to the purity–pollution criterion.

2. Cited in Irawati Karwe, 'What is Caste?', *Economic Weekly* 11, 1959, 157.

3. Stephen Fuchs, *At the Bottom of Indian Society: The Harijans and Other Low Castes* (New Delhi: Munshiram Manoharlal, 1981), 238. A newspaper story from South India reports the degradation heaped by the Dalits on a community which ranks even lower in the hierarchy. These are the Vannars who are forced to beg for food as a sign of their inferiority and degradation. 'Those defying the ancient hierarchy are repressed ruthlessly. There have been instances when Vannars in some villages have refused to beg for food. But they have either been forced to fall in line or driven out of the village'; cf. P.C. Vinoj Kumar, 'Wretched of the Earth', *Tehelka*, 13 August 2005.

4. L. Dumont, *Religion, Politics and History in India* (The Hague: Hague Press, 1970).

5. M.K. Gandhi, 'Untouchability and Swaraj', in *Collected Works of Mahatma Gandhi* (New Delhi: Publications Division, Government of India), vol. 28, 137. Hereafter referred to as *CWMG*.

6. Alan Dundes, *Two Tales of Crow and Sparrow* (Lanham: Rowman and Littlefield, 1997).

7. Vamik Volkan, 'An Overview of Psychological Concepts', in V.Volkan et al., eds., *The Psychodynamics of International Relationships* (Lexington: Lexington Books, 1990), 31–46.

8. M.K. Gandhi, 'Speech at Suppressed Classes Conference April 13, 1921', *CWMG*, vol. 23.

9. L. Kubie, 'The Fantasy of Dirt', *Psychoanalytic Quarterly* 6, 1937, 391.

10. Sheila Dhar, 'Siddheswari Devi: A Bird of Paradise', in *Here's Someone I'd Like You to Meet: Tales of Innocents, Musicians and Bureaucrats* (Delhi: Oxford University Press, 1996), 129–54.

11. Dumont, *Homo Hierarchicus*, 54. In relating dirt to caste hierarchy, the sociologist Milner also looks at dirt as something social rather than physical; cf. Murray Milner, *Status and Sacredness: A General Theory of Status Relations and an Analysis of Indian Culture* (New York: Oxford University Press, 1994).

12. D.W. Winnicott, *Collected Papers: Through Paediatrics to Psychoanalysis* (London: Taristock Publications, 1958), 34.

13. Durga Bhagvat, 'The Sparrow and the Crow', *Indian Folklore* 2, 1959, 213–5; cited in Dundes, op.cit., 32–3.
14. In *Uttara Ramayana* there is a story that once Yama, the god of death, was frightened by Ravana the king of demons and escaped in the form of a crow.
15. Béteille in P. Uberoi, ed., *Family, Kinship and Marriage in India*, 448–9.

## INDIAN WOMEN: TRADITIONAL AND MODERN

1. To take another example, the Indologist William Sax has shown that representations of characters in Hindu myths are more determined by caste than gender; see his 'Gender and the Representation of Violence in Pandava Lila', in J. Leslie & M. McGee, eds., *Invented Identities: The Interplay of Gender, Religion and Politics in India* (New Delhi: Oxford University Press, 2000), 252–64.
2. M. Pande, *Daughter's Daughter* (Delhi: Penguin, 1993), 85–6. The descriptions of growing up a girl in traditional India in this chapter are based on Kakar, *The Inner World*, 56–73, while some of the material on modern Indian women is from Kakar, 'Modernity and Female Childhood', in *Culture and Psyche: Selected Essays* (Delhi: Oxford University Press, 1997), 60–73.
3. A.A. MacDonell, *Vedic Religion*, 165; cited in R.M. Das, *Women in Manu and His Seven Commentators* (Varanasi: Kanchana Publications, 1962).
4. J.L. Roopnarine et al., 'Characteristic of Holding, Pattern of Play and Social Behaviors between Parents and Infants in New Delhi, India', *Developmental Psychology* 26(4), 1990, 667–73.
5. Pande, 45.
6. See for instance, L. Bennett et al., *Gender and Poverty in India: A World Bank Country Study* (Washington, D.C.: World Bank, 1991). The discrimination against the girl child holds true even for progressive states such as Tamil Nadu which has high levels of female literacy and work participation; see, T.K. Sundari Ravindran, 'Female Autonomy in Tamil Nadu', *Economic and Political Weekly*, April 17–24, 1999, WS34–44.

7. S. Anandalakshmy, ed., *The Girl Child and the Family* (Delhi: Dept. of Women and Child Development, Ministry of HRD, Government of India, 1994).

8. See Kakar, *The Inner World*, 60–1.

9. Pande, 45.

10. Kakar, *The Inner World*, 62.

11. 'The Laws of Manu', trans. G. Buhler, in M. Mueller, ed., *Sacred Books of the East*, vol. 25 (Oxford: Clarendon Press, 1886), 56. Hereafter referred to as *Manu*.

12. R.K. Verma and R. Ghadially, 'Mother's Sex-Role Attitudes and Demands', *Indian Journal of Social Work* 46(1), 1985, 105–11.

13. S.S. Luthar and D. Quinlan, 'Parental Images in Two Cultures: A Study of Women in India and America', *Journal of Cross Cultural Psychology* 24(2), 1993, 186–202.

14. In the *India Today* (20 February 2006) survey of urban youth, 71 per cent agree that divorce is better than a bad marriage.

15. L. Dube, *Anthropological Explorations in Gender: Intersecting Fields* (New Delhi: Sage, 2001).

16. Anandalakshmy, 66.

17. See M. Eapen and P. Kodoth, 'Family Structure, Women's Education and Work: Re-examining the High Status of Women in Kerala', in S. Mukhopadhyay and R.M. Sudarshan, eds., *Tracking Gender Equity and Economic Reform: Continuity and Change in South Asia* (New Delhi: Kali for Women, 2003), 227–67.

18. See Sundari Ravindran, WS34-44.

19. Ibid., WS-38.

20. In the feeling of well-being produced by the movie's happy end, we often fail to notice that the love marriage of the hero and heroine usually becomes an arranged one 'after the fact' when one or other sets of parents withdraw their opposition to the love match and both sets of parents come together at the end of the movie to bless the couple.

21. See S. Kakar and J.M. Ross, *Tales of Love, Sex and Danger* (New York: Blackwell, 1987), chap. 1.

22. Sundari Ravindran, WS-38.

23. See S. Kakar, *Intimate Relations: Exploring Indian Sexuality* (Chicago: University of Chicago Press, 1990), chap. 5.

24. G.N. Ramu, *Women, Work and Marriage in Urban India* (Delhi: Sage, 1990).

25. O. Kernberg, 'Love, the Couple, and the Group: A Psychoanalytic Frame', *Psychoanalytic Quarterly* 49, 1980, 78–108.

## SEXUALITY

1. M. Castleman, 'Review of Wendy Doniger and Sudhir Kakar's *Kamasutra: A New Translation* (London & New York: Oxford University Press, 2002)' in *Salon.com*, 29 May 2002. Much of the following is from the Introduction in the Doniger and Kakar book in which Doniger was very much the senior author. The quotes from the *Kamasutra*, in Doniger's translation, are from the same book.

2. R. Schmidt, *Beitreage zur Indischen Erotik. Das Liebesleben der Sanskritvoelker* (Berlin: Verlag Barsdorf, 1911), 1.

3. Kalidasa, *Kumara Sambhava*, in V.P. Joshi, ed., *The Complete Works of Kalidasa* (Leiden: E.J. Brill, 1976), 8.1.

4. *Manu*, 5.154.

5. *Kamasutra*, 6.3.41–3.

6. *Manu*, 9.15.

7. *Kamasutra*, 5.1.8.

8. Ibid., 2.10.6–13.

9. Kakar and Ross, *Tales of Love, Sex and Danger*, 202.

10. *Kamasutra*, 2.2.31.

11. Varahamira, *Brihatsamhita*, vol. 2, tr. M.R. Bhat (Delhi: Motilal Banarsidas), 74.20.

12. Jayadeva, *Gita Govinda*, tr., Barbara Stoler Miller (New York: Columbia University Press, 1977), 89.

13. A. Bouhdiba, *La Sexualite en Islam* (Paris: Presses Universitaires de France, 1975).

14. W. O'Flaherty, *Asceticism and Eroticism in the Mythology of Siva* (London: Oxford University Press, 1971), 51.

15. See S. Bott and S. Jejeebhoy, 'Adolescent Sexual and Reproductive Behavior: A Review of Evidence from India', in R. Ramasubban and S. Jejeebhoy, eds., *Women's Reproductive Health in India* (Jaipur: Rawat Publications, 2000), 40–101.

16. K. Poggendorf-Kakar, *Hindu Frauen zwischen Tradition und Moderne* (Stuttgart: Metzler Verlag, 2002), 81, 54.
17. Ibid., 82.
18. Kakar, *Intimate Relations*, op.cit., 20.
19. V. Geetha, 'On Bodily Love and Hurt', in M. John and J. Nair, eds., *A Question of Silence: The Sexual Economies of Modern India* (Delhi: Kali for Women, 1998), 304–31.
20. Kakar, *Intimate Relations*, 19.
21. Sundari Ravindran, WS-42.
22. M. Pande, *Stepping Out: Life and Sexuality in Rural India* (Delhi: Penguin, 2003).
23. Kakar, *Intimate Relations*, chap. 5.
24. M.E. Khan et al., 'Sexual Violence within Marriage', *Seminar* 447, 1996, 32–5, cited in S. Jejeebhoy and S. Bott, *Non-consensual Sexual Experiences of Young People: A Review of Evidence from Developing Countries* (Delhi: Population Council, 2003), 9. See also, A. George, 'Newly Married Adolescent Women: Experiences from Case Studies in Urban India', in S. Bott et al., eds., *Toward Adulthood: Exploring the Sexual Reproductive Health of Adolescents in South Asia* (Geneva: WHO, 2003), 67–70.
25. *Kamasutra*, 3.2.5-6.
26. This section is elaborated in greater detail in *The Inner World*, 87–103.
27. A.K. Ramanujan, 'The Indian Oedipus', in E. Lowell and A. Dundes, eds., *Oedipus: A Folklore Casebook* (New York: Garland, 1984), 254.
28. M.S. Gore, 'The Husband–Wife and Mother–Son Relationship', *Sociological Bulletin* 11, 1961, 91–102.
29. S.C. Dube, *Indian Village* (New York: Harper and Row, 1967), 190–7.
30. S. Asthana and R. Oostvogels, 'The Social Construction of Male Homosexuality in India: Implications for HIV Transmission and Prevention', *Social Science & Medicine* 52, 2001. See also J. Seabrook, *Love in a Different Climate: Men Who Have Sex with Men in India* (London: Verso, 1999).
31. Interview with Ashok Row Kavi, *http://gaytoday,badpuppy.com/garchive/interview/050399in.htm*

32. R. Vanita and S. Kidwai, eds., *Same-Sex Love in India* (New York: St Martin's Press, 2000), 28–30.
33. See Saleem Kidwai's Introduction to Part 3 of *Same-Sex Love in India*, 107–22.
34. This is especially true of precolonial Urdu poets. See T. Rahman, 'Boy Love in Urdu Ghazal', *Annual of Urdu Studies* 7, 1990, 1–20; C.M. Naim, 'The Theme of Homosexual (Pederastic) Love in Pre-Modern Urdu Poetry', in M.U. Memon, ed., *Studies in the Urdu Ghazal and Prose Fiction* (Madison: University of Wisconsin, 1979), 120–42.
35. D. Shastri, cited in Doniger and Kakar, *Kamasutra*, 35.

## HEALTH AND HEALING; DYING AND DEATH

1. A substantial part of this chapter is based on S. Kakar, *Shamans, Mystics and Doctors* (New York: Knopf, 1982), chap. 8, and S. Kakar, 'Health and Medicine in the Living Traditions of Hinduism', in L. Sullivan, ed., *Healing and Restoring: Health and Medicine in the World's Religious Traditions* (New York: Macmillan, 1989), 111–26.
2. G. Obeyesekere, 'The Theory and Practice of Psychological Medicine in the Ayurvedic Tradition', *Culture, Medicine and Psychiatry* 1, 1977, 155.
3. M. Bode, 'Taking Traditional Knowledge to the Market: The Commoditization of Indian Medicine', in *Anthropolgy and Medicine* 13:3, 2006, 225–36.
4. See also, T. Nisula, 'In the Presence of Biomedicine: Ayurveda, Medical Integration and Health Seeking in Mysore, South India', in *Anthropology and Medicine*, 13:3, 2006, 207–24.
5. Bode, op.cit.
6. The passage is adapted from Tarashankar Bandopadhyay's novel *Arogya Niketan* on an old Ayurvedic doctor's confrontation with the advent of Western medicine; see S. Kakar, 'Doctor at Large', *Illustrated Weekly of India*, 6 July 1986, 19–21.
7. Cited in Bode, op.cit.
8. A. Gopnik, 'Two Cooks', *The New Yorker*, 5 September 2005, 91–98.
9. Ibid., 97.

10. Cited in B. Das, 'A History of Ayurveda', *http://ayurveda-herbs.com*
11. There are a large number of studies in support of these conclusions. For older studies, see, for example, H. Ramachandran, *Environment, Health and Health Care System* (Bangalore, 1984); M.E. Khan and C.V.S. Prasad, *Health Seeking Behavior and Adoption of Family Planning in Himachal Pradesh* (Baroda: ORG, 1984). For newer studies documenting that nothing has changed in the last two decades, see M. Raina and S. Bonu, 'Rural Indian Women's Care Seeking Behavior and Choice of Provider for Gynecological Symptoms', in *Studies in Family Planning* 34:3, 2003, 175–85. For a comprehensive review of studies on the health care of poor children, see, S. Awasthi and S. Agarwal, 'Determinants of Childhood Mortality and Morbidity in Urban Slums in India', in *Indian Pediatrics* 40, 2003, 1145–61.
12. For an excellent review of the state of primary health care in India, see N. Bajpai and S. Goyal, *Primary Health Care in India: Coverage and Quality Issues* (Earth Institute, Columbia University, 2004).
13. Saumya Das, 'Epidemic Proportions', in *The American Prospect Online*, 29 July 2001.
14. Bhagavad Gita 2:27.
15. V. Das, 'Reflections on the Social Construction of Adulthood', in S. Kakar, ed., *Identity and Adulthood* (Delhi: Oxford University Press, 1979), 98.

## RELIGIOUS AND SPIRITUAL LIFE

1. A. Michaels, *Der Hinduismus: Geshichte und Gegenwart* (Hinduism: History and Present) (Munich: Beck Verlag, 1998), 17–8.
2. This section is largely based on S. Kakar, 'In Krishna's Mouth: Globalization and Hindu Nationalism', unpublished talk given at Centre for Study of Religions, Harvard University, October 2000.
3. See C. Jaffrelot, *The Hindu Nationalist Movement and Indian Politics* (New Delhi: Penguin, 1996).

4. V. Savarkar, *Hindutva* (1923) (Mumbai: Swatantrya Veer Savarkar Rashtriya Samarak, 1999).
5. Prerna, 'VHP Bares Fangs Against Conversion', *Tehelka.com*, 4 March 2001.
6. Vishwa Hindu Parishad, *The Hindu Awakening: Retrospect and Promise* (New Delhi: Vishwa Hindu Parishad, n.d.).
7. M.M. Joshi, 'Need for Selective Globalization', *Organizer*, 21 May 2000.
8. R. Grew, 'On Global History', unpublished ms. for the *Conference on Global History*, Bellagio, 16–21 July 1991.
9. K. Klostermeier, 'The Response of Modern Vaishnavism', in H.G. Coward, ed., *Modern Indian Responses to Religious Pluralism* (Albany: SUNY Press, 1987).
10. K.S. Sudarshan, Vijayadashmi Speech, in *Organizer*.
11. D. Idate, *Global Hindutva in the Twenty-first Century and Rashtriya Swayamsevak Sangh* (Mumbai: Hindu Vivek Kendra, 1997), 1.
12. A. Pandya, *Hindu Thought and World Harmony* (Bombay: Bharatiya Vidya Bhavan, 1989), 51–2.
13. See K. Poggendorf-Kakar, *Hindu Frauen Zwischen Tradition und Moderne* (Stuttgart: Melzer Verlag, 2002).
14. K. Poggendorf-Kakar, *Der Gottesmensch aus Puttaparthi* (Hamburg: Dr Kovacs Verlag, 1999). See also her *Adaption-Reinterpretation-Interdependenz: Postmoderne Religiositaet an Beispiel der Sathya-Sai Baba-Bewegung*, in M. Bergunder, ed., *Reinterpretation Hinduistischer Tradition in Kulturellen Kontext* (forthcoming).
15. Swami Vivekananda, *The Complete Works*, Mayavati Memorial Edition (Calcutta: Advaita Ashram, 1955), vol. 1, 331–2.
16. S. Gurumurthy, 'Unravel Truth through Debates', *Organizer*, 10 September 2000.

## CONFLICT: HINDUS AND MUSLIMS

1. M.K. Gandhi, 'Hindu–Muslim Tension: Its Cause and Cure', in *CWMG*, vol. 28, 65.
2. This chapter is substantially based on S. Kakar, *The Colors of Violence* (Chicago: University of Chicago Press, 1996).

3. See, for example, R.C. Majumdar, *Historiography in Modern India* (Bombay: Asia Publishing House, 1970).
4. Romila Thapar et al., *Communalism and the Writing of Indian History* (Delhi: People's Publishing, 1969).
5. G. Pandey, *The Colonial Construction of Communalism in North India* (Delhi: Oxford University Press, 1990).
6. N. Davis, *Society and Culture in Early Modern France* (Cambridge: Polity Press, 1987); G. Rude, *The Crowd in History: A Study of Popular Disturbances in France and England, 1848* (New York: Wiley, 1964); A.A. Engineer, ed., *Communal Riots in Post-Independence India* (Hyderabad: Sangam Books, 1985).
7. M. Walzer, 'Nations and Minorities', in C. Fried, ed., *Minorities: Community and Identity* (Berlin: Springer Verlag, 1982).
8. M. Marty and S. Appleby, eds., *Fundamentalisms Observed* (Chicago: University of Chicago Press, 1991).
9. A. Varshney and S. Wilkinson, *Hindu–Muslim Riots, 1960–93* (New Delhi: Rajiv Gandhi Institute of Contemporary Studies, 1996).
10. G. Krishna, 'Communal Violence in India', in *Economic and Political Weekly* 20, 1985, 117–31.
11. Gandhi, 'What May Hindus Do?' in *CWMG*, vol. 28, 183.
12. The quotes are from S. Kakar, *The Colors of Violence*, chaps. 4 and 5.
13. Dube, *Indian Village*, 187.
14. Kakar, *The Colors of Violence*, 137.
15. A.J. Dubois, *Hindu Manners, Customs and Ceremonies*, H.K. Beauchamp, ed. and trans. (Calcutta: Rupa, 1992), 218.
16. Kakar, *Shamans, Mystics and Doctors*, chap. 3.
17. Kakar, *The Colors of Violence*, 161.
18. Ibid.
19. M. Hasan, 'Minority Identity and its Discontents: Responses and Representations', paper read at International Congress of Asian Studies, Hong Kong, August 1993.
20. A. S. Ahmed, *Discovering Islam* (New Delhi: Vistaar Publications, 1990), 158–60. See also I. Ahmed, ed., *Modernization and Social Change among Muslims* (Delhi: Manohar, 1983).
21. Kakar, *The Colors of Violence*, 114–8.

22. Ibid., 161–2.
23. Ibid., 180.
24. Ibid., 165.
25. Ibid., 182.
26. Ibid., 184.
27. This section is adapted from S. Kakar, 'Rumors and Riots', in G. Fine et al., eds., *Rumor Mills* (Hawthorne, NY: Transaction, 2005), 53–60.
28. There is a judicial commission currently probing into what exactly happened.
29. Kakar, *The Colors of Violence*, 43.
30. E.H. Erikson, *Childhood and Society* (New York: Norton, 1952).
31. See Y. Gampel, 'The Role of Social Violence in Psychic Reality', in J. Ahumada et al., eds., *The Perverse Transference and Other Matters* (Northvale, New Jersey: Aronson, 1997).
32. M. Likierman, 'The Function of Anger in Human Conflict', *International Review of Psychoanalysis* 14:2, 1987, 143–62.
33. D. Horowitz, *The Deadly Ethnic Riot* (Berkeley: University of California Press, 2001), 545–55.

THE INDIAN MIND

1. For an elaboration of the Hindu world view see S. Kakar, *The Inner World*, chap. 2.
2. A.K. Ramanujan, 'Is There an Indian Way of Thinking?', in M. Marriott, ed., *India through Hindu Categories* (Newbury, California: Sage, 1990), 41–58.
3. F. Max Mueller, *India: What Can it Teach Us?* (New Delhi: Penguin, 2000).
4. *Manu*, 8:267.
5. Gautama, cited in Ramanujan, 'Is There an Indian Way of Thinking?', 46.
6. *Manu*, 8:352–62.
7. *Kamasutra*, Book 5.
8. R. Shweder and E.J. Bourne, 'Does the Concept of the Person vary Cross-Culturally?' in R. Shweder and R. LeVine, eds.,

*Culture Theory* (New York: Cambridge University Press, 1986), 158–99.

9. S. Kakar, *The Colors of Violence*, chap. 5.
10. S. Kakar, *The Inner World*, 44–5.
11. Ibid., 49
12. S. Kakar, 'Psychoanalysis and Non-Western Cultures', *International Review of Psychoanalysis* 12, 1985, 441–8.
13. The expression is by McKim Marriott; see his 'Hindu Transactions: Diversity without Duality', in B. Kapferer, ed., *Transactions and Meaning* (Philadelphia: Institute for the Study of Human Issues, 1976), 109–42.
14. Cited in R. Lannoy, *The Speaking Tree* (London: Oxford University Press, 1976), 78.
15. M. Franz, *Puer Aeternus: A Psychological Study of the Adult Struggle with the Paradise of Childhood* (Toronto: Inner City Books, 2000). We owe this reference and observation to David Johnston, 'A Comprehensive Approach to Psychotherapy', unpublished ms., November 2005.
16. See also B. Schaffner, 'Androgyny in Indian Art and Culture: Psychoanalytic Implications', *Journal of American Academy of Psychoanalysis* 29(1), 2000, 113–25.
17. See Kakar and Ross, *Tales of Love, Sex and Danger*, 99.

# INDEX

adultery, 72, 86, 94, 189
Agarwal community, 97
aggression, 69
Ahmedabad, Gujarat: Hindu-
    Muslim riots (1969), 166,
    169, 172
*Aitareya Brahmana*, 45
alchemy, 86–87
allopathy, 108, 112, 125–26
Amaru, 202
Ambedkar, Bhimrao R., 28–29
ancestral spirits, 110
Andalus syndrome, 161
animism, 134
antagonism, 168
anxiety, 16, 26, 57, 107, 108,
    171, 174
Arabs, 5, 28, 32
*ardhanarishwara*, 64, 202
Arya Samaj, 135
asceticism, ascetic imagination, 85–
    87, 90, 134
Asha Ram Bapu, 147
assimilation, transformation, re-
    assertion and recreation process,
    5, 140–41
Atharva Veda, 44
authority relations, 13–24
autointoxication theory, 112
autonomy: of the self, 201;
    unnatural, 197; of woman, 51
Avalokiteshwara, 202

Ayurveda, 4, 87, 107, 108, 110–
    11, 127, 132, 198;
    commercialization and
    standardization, 112;
    discourses on food, 121–23;
    idea about body, 125; illness
    in, 111–20
Azmi, Ubedullah Khan, 167–68

Babri Mosque, Ayodhya, 168;
    demolition (1992), 164, 166
Bajrang Dal, 138
beliefs and attitudes, belief system,
    26, 181, 182; cultural, 112;
    belief, 139; religious, 11, 136–
    37, 144, 152; social, about
    science of healing,111–12
Béteille, André, 39
*bhakti* (devotion), 83, 134, 145
Bharatiya Janata Party (BJP), 138,
    152
biomedicine and health, 125–27
biological infection, 109
body, bodily processes, 4, 132; as
    an animated, mobile dirt
    factory, 32–33, 35–36;
    consciousness, 92; contours,
    91–92; in health and illness
    in Ayurveda, 111–20; Hindu
    image, 111; *sharira*, 198, 199;
    connection with psyche, 111;
    Western tabbos, 33

body language, 19
Bollywood movies, 5, 62–63, 84, 181
Brahminism, 134
Brahmins, 34, 36, 131
Buddhism, 29

*Carakasamhita*, 118
caste, 1, 3, 4, 17, 22, 27, 41, 42, 189; and class barriers, 62; dirt and discrimination, 28, 29–40; evils, 39; and food habits, 35; and gender, 41; hierarchy, 25–29, 37, 40; identity, 40; inner experience, 25*ff*; considerations in marriage, 57
Catholic–Protestant violence in France, 154
celibacy, 85, 86, 87–89
Chandragupta Maurya, 3
*chapati*, 105–6
chastity, 90
Chaudhuri, Nirad C., 4
child, childhood, 2, 10–11, 15–17, 19, 22, 31–32; familiarity with the hierarchy of family organization, 14; role of tales and legends in shaping the mindset, 37–39; socialization, 194
Chinmayananda, Swami, 151
Christian(s), Christianity, 2, 6, 28, 135, 137, 140, 148, 149, 160; missionaries, 138; morality, 72
civilizational heritage, civilizations, 1, 5, 190
class, 1, 3, 61–62; *see also* middle class
cleanliness, western regimens, 33–36
co-education, 55
cohesion, 23
colonialism, 5, 153, 155

communal conflicts, communalism, 154, 162–63, 168, 172, 175–76, 177, 196
community-body, 163, 166, 170, 181
compassion, 163
conformity and conventional behaviour, 200
Confucian world view, 181
conjugal love, 73
connectedness, 196–201
conscience, 26
consciousness, 35, 40, 112, 123, 124, 128, 129, 177, 178, 182
consumerism, consumer culture, 57, 150
consummation, 80
context-sensitivity, 4, 188–89, 191, 203
contextualization, 124–25
conversion, 28, 138, 158
corporal punishment, 188–89
corruption, 16
cosmology, cosmos, 110, 111, 143, 181, 199
counter-enlightenment, 201
courtesans, 77
cow slaughter issue, 158
cross-cousin and uncle–niece marriages, 60
cultural, culture, 1–3, 21, 31, 54, 75, 89–90, 93, 111, 178, 182, 203; alienation, 139; and authority, 13–24; burden of fear, shame and guilt, 94; concepts, 148; conviction, 16; definition of marriage, 61; forces, 5; foundation, 137; gene pool, 4; heritage, 202, 203; ideals and values, 60, 101, 153, 155, 178, 197; identity, 139, 166; imagination of Indian women, 48, 64; pollution, 150; relativism, 62; view of the right action, 186–87; marked

preference for a son, 42–46; superego of Hindus, 88; *see also* Hindu, tradition

cynicism, 16

dalits and tribals, 6, 27, 30, 34; denied entry to temples, thoroughfares and other public spaces, 29; *see also* untouchables

daughter, daughterhood, 42–46, 56; *see also* girl child, women

daughter-in-law and mother-in-law relationship, 57–59, 97

death, 128–33; Hindu myth, 128–30

democracy, 26

demographic differences, 53

demographic perspective and Hindu–Muslim relations, 154

depersonalization as individual Hindus or Muslims, 163

*dharma*, 26, 103, 181, 185

dirt: and discrimination, 29–40; equation with dark colour, 36–39; Western fantasy, 33–34

discrimination, 5; against girl child, 47–49; and adolescent girls, 46–52; *see also* gender, women

disease, as a consequence of faulty distribution of bodily fluids, 112–13

disequilibrium (imbalance of *dosha*s), 110

domestic violence, 60

dowry, 57

Dumont, Louis, 1, 28; *Homo Hierarchicus*, 14, 21

economic factor, economy, 68; in family relationships, 9, 11; in Hindu–Muslim relations, 154, 176, 178; reason for the strong preference for male offspring, 45

egalitarianism, egalitarian ideology, 28, 30, 186

ego, 70

emotional, 170; access, 49; affinity, 20; conflicts, 56; contact, 203; gratification, 23; intensity, 174; needs and longings, 63; responses, 183; sustenance, 98; volatility, 53

empathy, 176–77, 203

endogamy, 26

environmental factors and illness, 114

Erikson, Erik, 170

Eros, 200

eroticism, 63, 70, 75–82, 85, 86, 94, 96, 97–98

ethical relativism, 186

ethnicity, 1, 3, 5, 174, 179

euphemism, 92

extended Indian family, duties and obligations, 70

fair skin, pan-Indian preference, 36–37

family, family bonds, family life, 1, 8–13, 18, 60, 63, 69, 131–32; and community, 201; hierarchy, 14–16, 18–19; ideology of, 4, 5; joint family, 4, 8–10, 20, 23, 49, 64, 67, 69; myths, 200; obligations, 12, 15, 62; status considerations in marriage, 57; values, 59; *see also* women

father–son relation, 23–24

favouritism, 20

fearfulness, 107, 108, 116

female, 105; agency, 55; community within family, 50; devaluation, 48; infant mortality, 47; infanticide and foeticide, 46–47; inheritance, 45; sexuality, 90, 99–100; *see also* girl child, gender, women

feminine values, femininity, 50, 52

Feng Shui, 148

fetishism, 149
filial devotion, 10, 16, 59
five elements (*panchabhuta*—earth, fire, wind, water and ether), 113, 121, 198; *see also* health
focal infection, concept of, 113
folk festivals, 196
folk wisdom, 54
food, food habits: dirty and impure, 35, 40; and Indian mind, 121–25; *see also* health
fundamentalism, 155, 177

Gandhi, M.K., 29, 32, 39, 88, 140, 152, 156, 159, 203
gender, 8, 41, 202; based dichotomy, 23; difference and discrimination, 48, 51, 60, 201–03; roles in sexual act, 81, 90
generational conflict, 15
girl child, discrimination against, 46–52
*Gita Govinda*, by Jayadeva, 83
globalization, 5, 134, 136, 139–41, 149, 150, 155
GLOBE (Global Leadership and Organizational Behaviour Effectiveness) study, 21, 22
Godhra, *see* Gujarat
Goethe, 42
Golden Temple, Amritsar, 146
guilt, 16, 17
Gujarat riots (2002), 168–69, 179

hadiths, 85
Haji Ali mosque, Mumbai, 146
health and healing, 107ff; and illness, 110, 111–20; and modern medicine, 125–27; and sexuality, 86–89
hell, Hindu concept of, 131
heterosexuality, 203
hierarchy, 7ff, 62; of caste, 25–29, 37, 40; internalization, 14
*hijra*s, 102

Hindu(s), Hinduism, 2, 4, 5, 6, 25, 28, 30, 32, 57, 71, 82, 86, 88, 103, 109–11, 129, 132, 134, 172, 182, 189; flexibility, 144–51; concern with food, 121, 125; identity, self-identification, 149–51, 157; Muslim conflict, 152ff; future, 177–79; image of the Muslim, 156–59; nationalists, 135–44, 149–50, 153, 166, 168, 173; relativism and inclusivity, 148; as a religion and Hindutva as a socio-political force, 137–38; religiosity, 82, 135; division into sects, 141; self-perception of being weak, 156; symbols, rituals and celebrations, 168, 178; traditional, 151; world view, 143, 180–96; worships, 167
holi, 196
homeopathy, 108
homoeroticism, 103
homogenization, 138, 163; of Hindu rituals and festivals, 147
homosexuals, 100–06; female, 105; male, 103–04
human existence, 180
human relationships, 72, 198
humane orientation, 21
humours, 113
Hutus, 32
Hyderabad: morality in violence among Hindus and Muslims, 175–76

ideals of womanhood, 52
identity, 1–2, 4, 6, 8, 11, 12, 23, 26, 27, 144, 155, 177; caste, 40; cultural, 139, 166; religious, 139, 160, 162, 164, 172, 174; sexual, 91, 101; social dimension, 25; of women, 56, 67, 69, 91

immune system, 114
Indian Penal Code, 104
individual and community, 196
individualism, 69, 79, 121, 201
in-group collectivism, 22
innate dispositions (*samskaras*),
    194–96
integrity, 152, 193
international relations, 155
interpersonal communion, 199
intuitive relationship with Divine,
    1, 134, 147
Islam, Islamic, 5, 28, 85, 103,
    140, 158, 160, 166, 172;
    identity, 168; and Judeo-
    Christian, 186; personal law,
    166; religious institutions, 138

Jains, 2

Kama (god of love), 88
*Kamasutra*, by Vatsyayana, 62,
    71–72, 75, 84–85, 95, 131,
    189; homosexuality, 104;
    lesbians, 105; love in age of,
    78–81; women in, 76–78
*karma* theory, 111, 128–29, 130–
    31, 148, 181; rebirth and the
    Indian mind, 193–96
Kashmir, militancy, 156
Khajuraho temples, Konarak, 76,
    81–82, 84, 85
kinship relations, 12, 14, 56
*kliba*, 102, 104
*Kumara Sambhava*, by Kalidasa,
    74

labour market, 66
Lama Fera, 148
leadership, 17–19, 22
lesbians, 104–06
*lex talionis*, 131
liberalization, 124, 136
love: in age of *Kamasutra*, 78–81;
    notion of, in sex, 77; *see also*
    marriage, sexuality

*Mahabharata*, 4, 73, 74, 191
Mahmud, Sultan of Ghazni, 173
male: cultural imagination, 93;
    dominance, 41; and female,
    201–03; psyche, 97; sexuality,
    90, 96–100
man's connection to the universe,
    201
Manu, 51, 188
marriage, institution of marriage,
    10, 12, 56–66, 68–69, 73;
    arranged, 62, 65; of a
    daughter, 56; inter-caste, 40;
    and kinship, 27, 56; love
    marriage, 61–62, 77; sexuality
    in, 93–96, 101; in South India,
    60; traditional Hindu, 57;
    ultimate goal is to develop
    love, 77; Western, 63
Marx, Karl, 154
maternal enthrallment, 98, 100
maternal sexuality, 99
matrilineal systems, 45, 60
medical theories, opinions and
    practices, 111, 125–27; *see
    also* health, Ayurveda,
    allopathy
meditation, 149
Megasthenes, 3
metabolic principles, 113
middle class, 7, 9–10, 12, 21, 146,
    149; orientations to caste, 39–
    40; girls/women, 42, 46, 51,
    52, 55, 57–59, 65–68, 69–70,
    90; marriages, 58; modernity,
    52; religious practices, 135,
    147; urban, 24, 39–40, 51,
    97, 112, 144; working
    women, 66
migrations and dislocations, 155
mind/body type, 113, 114
modernity, 24, 135, 145, 150, 183,
    186
modernization, 9, 12, 141, 144,
    155, 161, 179